A Pictorial History of Chinese Architecture

The MIT Press   *Cambridge, Massachusetts*   *London, England*

A Pictorial History of Chinese Architecture

Liang Ssu-ch'eng

A Study of the Development of Its Structural System and the Evolution of Its Types

Edited by Wilma Fairbank

Second printing, 1985
© 1984 by The Massachusetts
Institute of Technology

This book was set in Bembo and
Optima by Asco Trade Typesetting
Ltd., Hong Kong, and printed and
bound by Halliday Lithograph in the
United States of America.

The publisher wishes to thank the
following individuals who were
patrons of this edition: C. B. Sung,
Beulah Kwok Sung, J. S. Lee, and
W. Szeto.

Publication of this book has been
aided by a grant from Xerox
Corporation.

Library of Congress Cataloging in
Publication Data

Liang, Ssu-ch'eng, 1901–
   A pictorial history of Chinese
   architecture.

   Bibliography: p.
   Includes index.
   1. Architecture—China.
I. Fairbank, Wilma.   II. Title.
NA1540.L536 1984   720'.951
83-25607
ISBN 0-262-12103-4

To the memory of Liang Ssu-ch'eng, Lin Whei-yin, and their coworkers at

The Institute for Research in Chinese Architecture, whose perseverance through

times of disaster from 1931 to 1946 discovered a sequence of surviving

Chinese monumental structures and pioneered the scientific study of Chinese

architectural development

Contents

Foreword

Liang Ssu-ch'eng, a leading Chinese architect, was one of the founders of historical research on China's ancient architecture. He wrote this book during the Second World War shortly after completing his field investigations in North China and the interior. Professor Liang originally planned it to be one part of a large book, *The History of Chinese Art*. The other part, for which he had already written an outline, was to be on Chinese sculpture, but this plan was never carried out.

As it stands, the book is a valuable short summary of his early work and provides a brief visual survey of the great treasury of ancient Chinese architecture. One can study the "organic" structural system, the evolution of building types, and the development of various architectural elements by the comparative method. For the beginner it is a good introduction to the study of Chinese architectural history. The specialist, too, will draw inspiration from it. Liang never ceased searching for new understanding and is able to explain the profound in simple terms. Above all, the beautiful drawings from the skilled hands of Professor Liang and Mo Tsung-chiang provide a delightful esthetic experience for the reader.

Liang dedicated his life to architecture, and his contributions were many sided. Not only did he leave us many academic treatises and books in Chinese, which are going to be published or reprinted in Peking within the next few years, but he was also a respected and influential educator. He founded two architectural departments—one at Northeastern University, Liaoning Province, in 1928, and one at Tsing Hua University in 1946, which still flourishes. His students have spread all over China and work in a wide range of fields. From 1949 Liang participated in China's socialist reconstruction with heart and soul. He was appointed as one of the honored leaders in charge of designing the National Emblem of the People's Republic of China and, later, of the Monument of the People's Heroes. In addition, he did much useful work in planning the city of Peking and promoting historical conservation throughout China. Though Liang died more than ten years ago, he is still remembered with great respect and affection.

That this work will finally be published in the Western world as the author wished is especially due to the efforts of Liang's old friend Wilma Fairbank. After his death she helped us to find and recover the precious drawings that had been lost for more than twenty years and carefully shepherded the manuscript and many illustrations to their final form in this book.

Wu Liang-yong
Professor and Dean of the Architectural Department, Tsing Hua University
Member of the Technical Science Division, Chinese Academy of Sciences, Peking

Acknowledgments

Many admirers of Liang Ssu-ch'eng and of Chinese architecture have joined in the efforts to get his long-lost book into the hands of the Western readers for whom he intended it. Professor Wu Liang-yong, head of the Department of Architecture at Tsing Hua University, led the way when he asked me in 1980 to edit the manuscript and find an American publisher for it. I was happy to resume the responsibilities Liang had given me thirty-three years before.

When The MIT Press, long noted for the quality of its architectural books, accepted Liang's book for publication, the project was well started. However, the problems of editing such a complex volume across the Pacific loomed large. Unquestionably our basic good fortune was the whole-hearted cooperation of Liang's second wife, Lin Chu. She is a member of the Department of Architecture at Tsing Hua University, very cognizant of her husband's work, and devoted to his memory. We met in Peking in 1979 and worked together there in 1980 and 1982. In addition to performing her fulltime job, for three years she has shared with me endless details of checking, numbering, and labeling illustrations, supplied me with missing items, and answered my constant questions. Our airmail correspondence, she writing in Chinese, I in English, has been prompt and unceasing. She, a dear friend, deserves my primary gratitude.

After the text and illustrations were reunited in Peking in the summer of 1980, I spent time there on two occasions. The miraculous recovery of the lost materials opened many doors for me. My old friends, Liang's sister Liang Ssu-chuang, his son Liang Congjie and family, and his friend Chin Yueh-lin, were warmly welcoming and extremely helpful. I had the pleasure of interviewing and later corresponding with three elderly architects who had been Liang's classmates at Penn and his lifelong friends, Yang Ting-bao and Tung Chuin, both now deceased, and Chen Chih. Of the younger architectural historians who had participated in the 1930s field work of the Institute, I met Mo Tsung-chiang, Chen Ming-da, Lo Che-wen, Wang Shih-hsiang, and Liu Hsu-chieh, son and follower of Liu Tun-tseng. All had spent the war years in the southwestern provinces of Yunnan and Szechuan where the Institute took refuge. Some of the next younger generation, Liang's postwar students at Tsing Hua from the 1950s onward, have been particularly helpful during the final months of preparing the book for publication, especially Xi Shu-xiang, Yin Ye-ho, and Fu Xi-nian, as well as Fu's associate Sun Chen-fan in the China Building Technology Development Center in Peking. The glossary owes much to all four; Fu and colleagues sent some new photographs; and Xi made explanatory drawings for the editor's note and provided invaluable support in many other ways.

Sir Anthony Lambert and Tim Rock in London played important parts in recovering the lost illustrations. An important influence on me was Else Glahn of Aarhus University, Denmark, who is Europe's leading specialist in Chinese architecture. Sharing my admiration for Liang's work, she cooperated with me in pursuing it and I learned much from her long before beginning this book.

In America I have had generous help from the archivists of the University of Pennsylvania, Princeton, Yale, and Harvard. At Princeton, Robert Thorp and Huang Yun-sheng, a former student of Liang, have lent guidance and moral support. Friends at Yale have been unfailing: Jonathan Spence, Maryś Wright, Mary Gardner Neill, the architect King-lui Wu, and especially Helen Chillman to whom he directed me. She has charge of the unique collection of Chinese architecture slides made from Liang's prints for his 1947 lectures at Yale. Harvard being my home base, I have used the Harvard-Yenching Library and the Fogg Art Museum constantly. Eugene Wu, director of the former, and John Rosenfield, acting director of the latter, deserve my special thanks. William Coaldrake, historian of Japanese architecture, has managed to be always there when I needed him. Architects in the area have been very kind. I think especially of Paul Sun and David Handlin, who were advocates of the project from the first. Robin Bledsoe edited my editing, and my friend Joan Hill typed and retyped the manuscript. My sister Helen Cannon Bond gave me loving encouragement and practical assistance.

Foundation support from the American Philosophical Society and the National Endowment for the Humanities supported my research and travel. My trips to Peking were not only fruitful but joyous largely due to the hospitality of Arthur and Sheila Menzies and John and Michele Higginbotham of the Canadian Embassy.

My husband, John, stayed at home but that was his only vacation from the world of *tou-kung* that impinged on our lives as the book took shape. As always I thank him for his quiet confidence in me and the expert assistance he provided whenever I needed it.

Liang Ssu-ch'eng: A Profile

Liang Ssu-ch'eng at work,
around 1935

To us in the West the traditional architecture of China has long had the fascination of the exotic. Pagodas and temple buildings with their uptilted roofs, and the window latticework, garden moongates, and camelback bridges of palaces and residences so enchanted European designers of the early eighteenth century as to inspire the invention of "Chinoiserie." Chinese architectural motifs were depicted in wallpaper, painted on porcelain, imitated in furniture, and reproduced recognizably as outdoor features on the estates of the wealthy. This upper-class vogue perhaps reached its height in England in 1763 with the erection of the Kew Gardens pagoda and has never quite died away.

In China these architectural features had been developed by craftsmen over the centuries in response to basic needs, from simply providing shelter at one extreme to instilling religious piety or displaying imperial grandeur at the other. Slighted, for reasons still obscure, as the province of carpenters and masons, architecture did not evoke the intellectual curiosity that leads to scholarly analysis. Not until the twentieth century did the Chinese undertake the study of their own architectural history, and in this the pioneer was Liang Ssu-ch'eng (pronounced Leong Sss-chung).

By inheritance and training Liang (1901–1972) was superbly fitted to the role fate assigned him—leader of the first generation of Chinese architectural historians. He was the eldest son of the famous scholar-reformer Liang Ch'i-ch'ao, devoted to his father and highly impressionable. Knowledge of China's great traditions and its forward movements was deeply inculcated in the son. Liang was slight of stature and by nature observant, curious, careful, and aesthetically sensitive. He loved to draw and was talented musically. Though he had been born in Tokyo where his father was a temporary political refugee, he grew up in Peking. There he received his initial preparation in the two educational spheres that would prove vital for his future achievements. These were, first, the traditional training, supervised by his father, in classical Chinese that he would need for studying old books and deciphering stelae inscriptions, and, second, a firm grounding in English language, Western sciences, and humanities at Tsing Hua College, specifically designed to prepare students for further study abroad. He and his schoolmates were of that remarkable generation of Chinese intellectuals, bilingual and bicultural, who achieved the miracle of bridging the gap between East and West.

Chance played its part in Liang's choice of architecture as a career. It was suggested by the girl who was later to become his wife, Lin Whei-yin, daughter of Lin Ch'ang-min, a scholar-diplomat and well-known poet. When Lin Ch'ang-min was sent to London on an assignment in 1921, he took his daughter along for company. She was barely seventeen, very bright, quick, and pretty, and already beginning to evidence the magnetism that was to draw others to her irresistibly throughout the years ahead. She had her father's gift for writing poetry but was equally attracted to the other arts, particularly drama, drawing, and painting. Enrolled in a British girls' school, she quickly developed her knowledge of English to unusual facility in both speaking and writing. From a British schoolmate who played at designing houses, she learned of the profession of architect. Attracted to a lifework that combined daily artistic creativity with immediate usefulness, she decided this was the profession she wanted. On her return to China she easily won Liang to the same decision.

Both Liang and Lin Whei-yin decided to study at the University of Pennsylvania Department of Architecture headed by the eminent Paul Cret from the Ecole des Beaux Arts in Paris. Liang's entry was delayed until the fall term of 1924 by a disastrous motorcycle accident in Peking in May 1923 that caused multiple fractures of his left leg. It never healed properly and remained slightly shorter than his right. As a young man, Liang was strong and active despite this handicap, but in later years it affected his spine and he sometimes suffered intense pain.

The curriculum at Penn, based on the Beaux-Arts tradition, was designed to produce practicing architects but was equally well suited to prepare architectural historians. Students were required to study the classical orders of Greece and Rome and the monuments of medieval and Renaissance Europe. Their skills were tested by such challenging assignments as drafting restorations of ancient ruins or completing the designs of unfinished cathedrals. A basic requirement was the development of clear and beautifully executed architectural rendering, including the necessary lettering. Liang excelled in this and later required the same high level of performance from his young coworkers and students.

During his second year at Penn, Liang received from his father in Peking a book that was destined to affect his entire life. It was a key to Sung dynasty architecture, the *Ying-tsao fa-shih* (*Building Standards*), compiled in 1103 by a brilliant official at the Sung court, which set forth in unfamiliar terminology the techniques of Sung construction. It had essentially disappeared in succeeding centuries but a manuscript copy had recently been discovered and published. Liang tackled the book at once but, he admitted later, understood very little. Beforehand he had apparently given little thought to Chinese architectural history, but from now on the challenge to solve the obscurities of this key work was fixed in the back of his mind.

Lin Whei-yin reached Penn also for the fall term of 1924, only to discover that women were not admitted to the Department of Architecture. She enrolled in the university's School of Fine Arts, managed to take courses in architecture and, in fact, in 1926 was appointed "Part-Time Assistant to the Architectural Design Staff." The following year she was elevated to "Part-Time Instructor." In June 1927 she received the Bachelor of Fine Arts degree with honors at the same ceremony in which Liang was awarded with similar distinction the degree of Master of Architecture.

After a summer spent working in Cret's office in Philadelphia, the pair parted for a few months to pursue separate studies. Lin Whei-yin's long interest in drama led her to Yale to study stage design at George P. Baker's famous workshop. Liang went to Harvard to study the writings of Western scholars on Chinese art and, if possible, architecture.

At just this period, when Liang was in his mid-twenties, the first books seriously devoted to Chinese architecture appeared in the West. A German, Ernst Boerschmann, published two volumes of photographs of characteristic Chinese building types in 1923 and 1925. Two treatises by the Swedish art historian Oswald Sirén on the city walls, gates, and palaces of Peking appeared in 1924 and 1926. Much later, from hindsight, Liang commented, "Neither knew the grammar of Chinese architecture; they wrote uncomprehending descriptions of Chinese buildings. But, of the two, Sirén was the better. He used the newly recovered *Ying-tsao fa-shih*, though carelessly."

The wedding of Liang and Lin Whei-yin, deferred at his father's urging until both had completed their studies, took place in March 1928 in Ottawa, where Liang's elder sister was living as wife of the Chinese Consul-General. The young couple left at once for a grand tour of Europe on their way home. Rushing by car from place to place to see in a limited time everything they had studied, they "covered" England, France, Spain, Italy, Switzerland, and Germany. It was the first of the many architectural field trips they were to share in the years to come. In midsummer they were suddenly called home by word of an important job opening for Liang. Only then did they learn of the serious illness of Liang's father, who was shortly to suffer an untimely death in January 1929.

Young Liang was appointed in September 1928 to establish and head a Department of Architecture at Northeastern University in Shenyang, then known to Westerners as Mukden, Manchuria. With the help of his wife and two other Chinese architects from Penn, he set up a Cret-style curriculum and an architectural design firm. China's vast northeast was a still underdeveloped territory of great potential wealth. The demand for architectural design and construction appeared limitless, save for the menace of Japanese militarism. The young architects were soon busy with teaching, city planning, designing, and supervising construction. But in September 1931, three years after Liang had joined the university faculty, a Japanese military coup seized control of the northeastern provinces. It was the completion of the first stage of Japanese aggression in China, which was to continue for the next fourteen years, exploding into armed conflict in 1937.

This autumn of blighted hopes marked a decisive turn in Liang's career. He had accepted in June a new position, which led to his spending his most productive years as an architectural historian. The Society (later Institute) for Research in Chinese Architecture had been established in Peking in 1929 by a wealthy retired official, Chu Ch'i-ch'ien, as a consequence of his discovery of the *Ying-tsao fa-shih*. Its recovery and reprinting at his initiative had caused a sensation in scholarly circles. Hoping to unlock its mysteries, he had assembled a small bookish staff but, since neither they nor he had training in architecture, Chu had for some months been urging Liang to join the Society to direct its research.

The Society's headquarters were rooms just inside the Tien An Men on the west side of the courtyard. There in the autumn of 1931 Liang resumed his earlier study of the Sung manual. It seemed so promising, yet most of the technical terms still eluded him. His practical training and experience told him, as he expressed it, that "the only reliable sources of information are the buildings themselves and the only available teachers are the craftsmen." He conceived the idea of starting his research by studying the construction of the palace buildings around him under the tutelage of certain old carpenters who had spent their lives maintaining them. Most of the buildings had been erected in the Ch'ing (Manchu) dynasty (1644–1912). A Ch'ing handbook of structural regulations, the *Kung-ch'eng tso-fa tse-li*, had been published in 1734. It was filled with equally unfamiliar technical terms, but the old craftsmen knew orally the traditional terms, and with their guidance Liang was able to identify the various timbers and other structural parts, to observe the complex building methods, and to decipher the regulations cited in the manual. This firsthand research resulted in his first book, *Ch'ing-tai ying-tsao tse-li* (Ch'ing Structural Regulations), which discussed and explained the Ch'ing manual (although in Liang's view it was not in the same class as the 1103 Sung manual).

In this way Liang achieved his first insights into what he called "the grammar of Chinese architecture." He was still puzzled and challenged by the *Ying-tsao fa-shih*, with its data about eleventh-century buildings. But experience had convinced him that the key was to find and examine surviving buildings of that period. The time had come for wide-ranging field trips.

The Liang's European honeymoon had been a field trip of a sort, to see firsthand the architectural monuments already studied from secondary sources at Penn. His months of scrutiny of Ch'ing architecture with the carpenters in Peking had resembled the firsthand inspection of field trips without the travel. It was obvious that further comprehension of the grammar of Chinese architecture and of its evolution must depend upon collecting a corpus of extant dated structures of earlier periods that had remained as far as possible in their original condition.

Liang's special interest in field investigations was recognized by the Society, which named him Director of Technical Studies, in 1931. A coordinate position, Director of Documentary Studies, was given the next year to a newcomer, Liu Tun-tseng, a very able scholar a few years older than Liang who had received his architectural training in Japan. The two men worked harmoniously together as a mutually supportive team leading their younger colleagues through the following decade. Inevitably, each did both documentary research and field studies because the two aspects of the work were fundamentally inseparable.

Where were the surviving buildings of pre-Ch'ing date to be found? Relatively few remained in the big cities. Many had been destroyed carelessly by fire or conflict, others intentionally by dynastic or religious enemies. The search had to explore the smaller towns in the countryside and remote temple complexes in the hills. Before undertaking such expeditions, the Liangs learned to map out their routes on the basis of local gazetteers. These scholarly compilations of local history noted the ancient temples, pagodas, and other monuments in which each district took pride. But the dates were not necessarily reliable, and often buildings that sounded like treasures and inspired long side trips were discovered to have been drastically altered or demolished. Nevertheless, these guidebooks provided the means of surveying wide areas, eventually whole provinces, without missing whatever important structures had survived. Of course, certain individual discoveries resulted from pursuing rumors, word-of-mouth suggestions, even obscure monuments praised in traditional folksongs. In the 1930s the field of Chinese architectural history was truly open to the excitement of unprecedented finds.

The same period put serious difficulties in the way of the investigators. Travel, if begun by train, was usually followed by crowded bus over rutted roads, ending often by mule-drawn, two-wheeled springless Peking cart. Precious gear had to be transported—cameras, tripods, measuring tapes, and other paraphernalia, including the indispensable note-books. Lodging had to be found in temples or in local inns, where commonly disease-carrying lice thrived and outhouses teemed with maggots. Roadside teahouses often provided delicious simple fare, but the cleanliness of chopsticks, bowls, and any cold or uncooked food was dubious. In certain areas of North China there was also the risk of attack by bandits who preyed on unsuspecting travelers.

The Liangs traveled together whenever Lin Whei-yin could safely leave their two small children. A younger colleague, often Mo Tsung-chiang who had been trained by Liang, usually accompanied them, as well as a man servant to handle baggage and local errands. Telephones were few. The local yamen or headquarters might have one as a link with superiors elsewhere, but there were rarely lines within a town itself. Thus much time was consumed in finding and negotiating with local officials, Buddhist dignitaries, and others before an exciting discovery could be examined.

When at last all these obstacles were overcome, the small team set to work. They used metric tapes to measure both large and small components of the structure, as well as its immediate setting. These measurements, and notebook sketches, would be necessary for later making ground-plan, elevation, and section drawings, and in very special cases for making three-dimensional models. Meanwhile Liang himself was climbing over the structure with his Leica camera, taking photographs of significant details to add to his previously snapped general views. Both measuring and photographing often required erecting temporary scaffoldings, disturbing bats and the dust of ages. The inscriptions on the stone stelae standing in the temple courtyards or porches, which recorded the dates and circumstances of the erection or repair of the building, had to be painstakingly copied, often by Lin Whei-yin. All this precious information was set down in notebooks and carried back to Peking for processing and publication.

Liang's first field trip, made in 1932, resulted in one of his greatest discoveries. It was the towering Buddhist structure, Tu-le Ssu, located sixty miles east of Peking, which housed a clay figure fifty-five feet high. Both the wood-frame building, erected in 984, and the statue had survived almost a thousand years in good condition.

In 1941 Liang summarized in unpublished notes the strenuous field explorations of the thirties:

For the last nine years, the Institute for Research in Chinese Architecture of which I am a member has been dispatching twice every year, on trips of two or three months' duration, small teams of field workers headed by a research fellow to comb the country for ancient monuments. The ultimate aim is the compilation of a history of Chinese architecture, a subject that has been virtually untouched by scholars in the past. We could find little or no material in books; we have had to hunt for actual specimens.

We have, up till today, covered more than 200 *hsien* or counties in fifteen provinces and have studied more than two thousand monuments. As head of the Section of Technical Studies, I was able to visit most of these places personally. We are very far from our goal yet, but we have found materials of great significance.

For the Liangs, the high point of their years of searching was the discovery in June 1937 of a Buddhist temple, Fo-kuang Ssu, built in 857 A.D. This beautiful structure, located deep in the mountains of northern Shansi province, had endured in good condition for over a thousand years and was recognized by Liang to be the oldest wooden building yet discovered in China and the first one of T'ang date. His description of it on pages 43–44, though brief, betrays his special love for this "treasure of the first order."

A remarkable aspect of the work of the Society in the 1930s was the speed and thoroughness with which the architectural discoveries were published in the Society's quarterly bulletin, *Chung-kuo ying-tsao hsueh-she hui-k'an*. The articles, in Chinese, described the buildings in detail and illustrated them with numerous photographs and drawings. Tables of contents were listed in English. Unfortunately, copies of the seven volumes of the bulletin are rare today.

This book was written by Liang during the final years of World War II in the remote and backward Yangtze river town of Li-chuang, Szechuan. He and his family, with some members of the Society, had left Peking in the summer of 1937 as the city was falling to the Japanese. They made their way in the great refugee migration to the mountain-ringed southwestern provinces, which were still controlled by the Chinese government. There the Society was made an Institute of the National Academy, Academia Sinica, with Liang in charge. Surveys of the architecture of Yunnan and Szechuan were undertaken. But as the eight years of war, isolation, and soaring inflation continued, illness and poverty worsened. Liu Tun-tseng left to join National Central University in Chungking, and younger members of the group scattered in their own interest. Liang remained in Li-chuang with his family, his faithful assistant, Mo Tsung-chiang, and a few others. Lin Whei-yin was confined to bed with tuberculosis. It was in such circumstances that Liang, in 1946, with his wife's help as always, composed this, his only book written in English, to acquaint the outside world with the achievements of the Institute for Research in Chinese Architecture during the previous fifteen years.

Emerging from isolation and privation at the end of the war, Liang received in 1946 cordial invitations from both Princeton and Yale universities to revisit the United States and lecture on Chinese architecture. His Chinese publications had reached the West, and he was now a scholar of international reputation. He settled his family in Peking and accepted the Yale appointment as visiting professor for the spring term of 1947. It was to be his second and last visit to the United States.

Thus far I have written this account impersonally, since its purpose is to present Liang and Lin Whei-yin in their important leadership roles without intrusion. But much of what I have written above I know firsthand from a close friendship with the Liangs, which has a bearing on this story. My husband and I were young newlywed students in Peking in the summer of 1932 when mutual Chinese friends introduced us to the Liangs. They were several years older, but their student years in America were not very far in the past. Perhaps that prompted our immediate liking for each other. They were neighbors as well as friends, and we all shared interests in Chinese art and history. For whatever reasons, we became intimates in the next four years of our stay in Peking. Liang, at the time we met, had just completed his first field trip. Two years later they visited us in an old mill in Shansi, which we had rented for the summer, and we had the unforgettable experience of accompanying them on a long field trip into hitherto unexplored territory. We shared with them the primitive travel conditions, the excitement or disappointment at the end of promising side trips to look for buildings described in the old gazetteers, and the interesting tasks of making measurements. Our friendship continued by correspondence after our return to America, and it deepened when we returned to China in government service during World War II. At that time we, as well as they, were in the far west of China while the Japanese armies occupied Peking and the entire east coast.

A visit to the Liangs in Li-chuang was a revelation to us of the poverty and misery induced by the war. Yet under these conditions Liang, who was nurse and cook as well as research director, was writing a detailed history of Chinese architecture in Chinese as well as the shorter *Pictorial History*. To illustrate these works he and his draftsmen were preparing from photographs and field-trip measurements some seventy large drawings—plans, elevations, and sections—of the most important architectural monuments they had studied. The drawings, reproduced here, are unquestionably fundamental contributions by Liang to our understanding of the history of Chinese architecture.

When the eight years of war ended, Liang discovered that the negatives of the Leica photographs that he and his coworkers had taken on their field trips had been destroyed by floods in the Tientsin bank where they had been left for safekeeping when the group went as refugees to the west. Only the prints that he had taken with him remained.

When Liang came to Yale in 1947, he brought the photographic prints, the superb drawings, and the text of his *Pictorial History* in the expectation of finding a publisher. He was kept busy with teaching at Yale, lecturing and receiving an honorary degree at Princeton, and consulting on the design of the UN headquarters with a small group of internationally known architects. In moments snatched here and there he and I worked on his text. In June 1947 he suddenly received word that Lin Whei-yin must have a serious operation, and he departed for Peking at once. Leaving the drawings and photographs with me, he took the sole copy of the text with him "to finish on the long trip home" and mail back to me. It never came.

Alarm and grief at the crisis in his wife's precarious health were enough to distract Liang. The family's personal concerns were soon submerged by the tumultuous events of the revolution and the remaking of Chinese life. In 1950 the newly established People's Republic of China turned to Liang for counsel and leadership in rebuilding, city planning, and other architectural matters. Even the gravely ill Lin Whei-yin participated in designing at the request of the government before her early death in 1954.

Perhaps it was the shock of her death that turned Liang's thoughts back to his long-abandoned project. He sent for the package of illustrations he had left behind. I mailed them at his direction to the address of a student in England for forwarding to him. A letter from the addressee confirmed that they reached England safely and in good condition in April 1957. Not until the autumn of 1978 did I discover that they had never reached Liang, who had died in 1972 after years of influential teaching at Tsing Hua University but without the opportunity to publish his research findings illustrated by the relevant drawings and photographs.

This book is the happy ending of the story. In 1980 the lost package of illustrations was miraculously recovered. A British friend in London managed to trace for me the student's current whereabouts and turn up an address in Singapore. There lay the package, untouched, on a shelf. After some negotiation it was sent off to Peking and reunited with Liang's text in the Department of Architecture of Tsing Hua University. Though its publication has been delayed for over thirty years, Liang's *Pictorial History of Chinese Architecture* brings to Western scholars, students, and general readers the architectural discoveries and insights of China's outstanding pioneer in this field.

Wilma Fairbank
Cambridge, Mass.

Editorial Method

As editor of this book, I have observed certain self-imposed constraints necessitated by the strange history of the manuscript. Fundamental, of course, is the fact that Liang, who wrote it in the 1940s, died more than a decade before its publication. Had he lived he might well have rewritten and expanded certain parts, notably his very brief comments on bridges, tombs, and other constructions that follow his fuller treatment of timber-frame buildings and pagodas. In the circumstances, my responsibility was to be scrupulously faithful to his ideas, and as far as possible to his choice of words, without making extraneous alterations in the typescript that he left. My one interpolation is clearly identified (pp. 11–12).

When Liang decided to present to Western readers a summary of the discoveries made by the Institute for Research in Chinese Architecture during its 1931–1937 studies and explorations in North China and its 1938–1946 wartime refuge in Yunnan and Szechuan, he settled on a pictorial history—not of all Chinese architecture as the title might imply but of important monuments of North China and of relevant examples from other provinces studied by the Institute. He intended to tell his story through selected photographs of historic structures from the Institute's files, interpreted by means of drawings showing their plans, elevations, and sections based on field measurements. Instead of an accompanying text, identifications and brief comments in Chinese and English were to be lettered on the drawings themselves.

The drawings were completed as planned in 1943. Liang took them from Li-chuang, Szechuan, downriver to Chungking where friends in the American Office of War Information photo lab recorded them for him on two reels of microfilm. He sent me one reel for wartime safekeeping, which I deposited in the Harvard-Yenching Library. When he brought the original drawings to America in 1947 he left the second reel in China. This precaution was to have interesting results.

Meanwhile, Liang admits, "after the completion of the drawings it seemed that a few words of explanation might be necessary." The text, which sets forth his analyses and conclusions based on his years of unprecedented field studies, is brief but deals with a surprisingly large number of structures. The brevity precludes consideration of many aspects of Chinese architecture that Liang treats in his Institute *Bulletin* articles on the same buildings. The headings by period reflect his evaluations at the time of writing. That time was nearly forty years ago, but the book has long been needed, and rather than distort it by updating, it seems best to preserve and present it as a historic document. Two draft pages on imperial gardens at the end have been omitted as incomplete and remote from the theme of structural development.

Liang wrote in clear, simple English and introduced important Chinese architectural terms in Wade-Giles romanization, which is retained, with a few exceptions for proper names varied by personal choice. The glossary of technical terms reminds the reader of their meanings and provides the Chinese characters. This bilingual feature has a prime significance. The captions lettered on the drawings in both languages imply that serious Western students of Chinese architecture must become familiar with technical terms and the names of monuments and localities in Chinese. Liang at Penn learned the analogous English and French terms for Western architectural history, to which he added his own hard-won knowledge of Chinese architectural history. Similarly, future generations of students in the West who will travel easily and often to China will need to know both its language and its hitherto neglected art of architecture.

Most of the photographs show the monuments in their condition in the 1930s. A few buildings reported to be no longer existing are identified in their captions as "Destroyed"— whether by deterioration, accident, or intent, we are not sure. In the hand-lettered drawings minor mistakes in English words, romanizations, or dynasty dates are intentionally left unaltered. It is unfortunate that Liang, beset by personal problems, did not end his text with a summation in 1947. But his "evolution" drawings (figs. 20, 21, 32, 37, 38, 63), which are here published for the first time, clearly summarize key developmental changes that he traced throughout the text. Others of the drawings have been published in the last thirty years in both East and West without attribution to Liang or the Institute. The source is Liang's second 1943 microfilm reel, which was reproduced in 1952 in a *nei-pu* (internal use only) pamphlet for Tsing Hua architecture students. Copies are known to have reached Europe and Britain. No text was attached so perhaps plagiarism cannot be alleged, but the publication of this book must bring the practice to an end.

Maps: Locations of Monuments Mentioned in Liang's Text

Certain recurrent geographical terms are easily learned. Province names often include *nan*: south, *pei*: north, *tung*: east, *hsi* (or *si*): west. East-flowing rivers, *ho* (e.g., Yellow or Yangtze), have provinces bordering on the north (Hopei) or south (Honan). Mountains, *shan*, may have provinces on their east (Shantung) or west (Shansi).

Boundaries, place names, and the North China railway network are shown as they were in the 1930s at the height of Liang's architectural explorations.

OUTER MONGOLIA

MANCHURIA

• Shenyang (Mukden)

INNER MONGOLIA

Yellow River

• Peking

• Tat'ung

KOREA

Tun-huang

NINGHSIA

Tientsin •

Taiyuan •

HOPEI

• Seoul

SHANSI

Yellow River

KANSU

SHENSI

Fen River

• Tsinan

SHANTUNG

Yellow Sea

Yellow River

Wei River

Yellow River

• Loyang

K'aifeng •

KIANGSU

Sian •

HONAN

SZECHUAN

ANHWEI

• Nanking

Kuan Hsien •

Chü Hsien •

HUPEI

• Shanghai

• Kuanghan

Chengtu •

• Soochow

Chiang-k'ou •

• Wuhan

Omei Shan

Min River

I-pin •

• Chungking

Tang-yang •

Hangchow •

East China Sea

Chin-hua •

Li-chuang •

• Wu-i

• Hsuan-p'ing

Tali

Changsha •

KIANGSI

CHEKIANG

Fumin •

HUNAN

Kunming

KWEICHOW

FUKIEN

• Foochow

YUNNAN

KWANGSI

KWANGTUNG

Ch'uanchou •

Chin-chiang

Amoy

TAIWAN

Formosa Strait

Canton •

VIETNAM

Hong Kong

South China Sea

Gulf of Tonkin

HAINAN

Miles 0   100   200   300   400

Kilometers 0   200   400

LIAONING

INNER MONGOLIA

Ch'ao-yang •

JEHOL

Shenyang
(Mukden)

I Hsien •

Yellow River

Great Wall

Tat'ung •

• Yun-kang

Ch'ang-p'ing

• Chi Hsien

• Ying Hsien

Fang Shan

Peking

• Tai Hsien

Cho Hsien •

• Pao-ti

Wu-t'ai Shan

I Hsien •

Ting-hsing

Tientsin

SHANSI

Ch'u-yang •

HOPEI

Hsing-t'ang •

• Ting Hsien

Taiyuan

Cheng-ting

Chin-tz'u

Yu-t'zu

• Chao Hsien

SHENSI

Fen-yang •

Hsing-t'ai

Tsinan

• Ch'ang-ch'ing

Tz'u Hsien •

Yellow River

Fei-ch'eng

SHANTUNG

Yellow Sea

Chao-ch'eng •

• Lin-fen

Anyang

Ch'ü-fu

• Hsin-chiang

Tsining •

• Chia-hsiang

• Ching-yang

Hsiu-wu

Chin-hsiang

Loyang

Sung Shan

K'aifeng

• Sian

Teng-feng •

KIANGSU

HONAN

ANHWEI

Miles	0		100		200		300		400

Kilometers	0		200		400	

A Pictorial History of Chinese Architecture

Liang Ssu-ch'eng

A Study of the Development of Its Structural System and the Evolution of Its Types

Preface

This volume is by no means an all-inclusive history of Chinese architecture. It is an attempt to present, by means of photographs and drawings of many typical specimens, the development of the Chinese structural system and the evolution of its types. My first intention was to do without any text. But after the completion of the drawings, it seemed that a few words of explanation might be necessary.

The Chinese building is a highly "organic" structure. It is an indigenous growth that was conceived and born in the remote prehistoric past, reached its "adolescence" in the Han dynasty (around the beginning of the Christian era), matured into full glory and vigor in the T'ang dynasty (seventh and eighth centuries), mellowed with grace and elegance in the Sung dynasty (eleventh and twelfth centuries), then started to show signs of old age, feebleness, and rigidity, from the beginning of the Ming dynasty (fifteenth century). Though it is questionable how much longer its lifeblood can be kept flowing, throughout the thirty centuries encompassed in this volume the structure has retained its organic qualities, which are due to the ingenious and articulate construction of the timber skeleton where the size, shape, and position of every member is determined by structural necessity. Thus the study of the Chinese building is primarily a study of its anatomy. For this reason the section drawings are much more important than the elevations. This is an aspect quite different from the study of European architecture, except perhaps the Gothic in which the construction governs more of the exterior appearance than in any other style.

Now, with the coming of reinforced concrete and steel framing, Chinese architecture faces a grave situation. Indeed, there is a basic similarity between the ancient Chinese and the ultramodern. But can they be combined? Can the traditional Chinese structural system find a new expression in these new materials? Possibly. But it must not be the blind imitation of "periods." Something new must come out of it, or Chinese architecture will become extinct.

A study of Chinese architecture would be incomplete without reference to Japanese architecture, for certain early phases of Japanese architecture should properly be classified as Chinese exports. However, this brief text can only touch upon the subject.

The reader should not be surprised that the overwhelming number of architectural examples presented here are Buddhist temples, pagodas, and tombs. In all times and all places religion has provided the strongest impetus to architectural creation.

The materials in this volume are chosen almost entirely from the files of the Institute for Research in Chinese Architecture. Some of them have been published in the bulletin of the Institute. Since its foundation in 1929, under the inspiring guidance of Mr. Chu Ch'i-ch'ien, President, and Dr. Y. T. Tsur, Acting President during the war years, 1937–1946, the Institute has been engaged in systematically searching the country for architectural specimens, studying them from both the archaeological and geographical points of view. So far, more than two hundred *hsien* (districts) in fifteen provinces have been covered. Had it not been for the interruption of the war, during which field work was almost entirely suspended, we would have a much richer collection to present. I am further handicapped by the fact that as I write, in far western Szechuan, many of my materials are not at hand. They were left in Peking when the Institute moved to the hinterland. Meanwhile, a number of the buildings presented here must have been lost forever as a result of the war. The extent of damage can be ascertained only by the reexamination of each individual monument.

The materials of the Institute were collected during numerous field trips, conducted either by Professor Liu Tun-tseng, formerly Director of the Documentary Section of the Institute, and now Chairman of the Department of Architecture and Dean of the College of Engineering, National Central University, or by myself. I am most grateful to Mr. Liu for his permission to use some of his materials in this volume. I am indebted to my colleague, Mr. Mo Tsung-chiang, Associate Research Fellow of the Institute, who accompanied me on almost every one of my field trips, for making most of the plates.

To Dr. Li Chi, Chairman of the Section of Archaeology of the Institute of History and Philology, Academia Sinica, and Mr. Shih Chang-ju, Associate Research Fellow of the same Institute, I am thankful for their permission to reproduce a drawing of the Shang–Yin site at the Anyang excavations; and to Dr. Li again, as Director of the National Central Museum, for his permission to use some of the materials excavated in the Han tombs at Chiang-k'ou, in which the Institute for Research in Chinese Architecture participated.

To my friend and colleague, Wilma Fairbank, member of the Institute for Research in Chinese Architecture, who has traveled extensively in China and participated in one of my field trips, I am indebted not only for the reconstruction of the shrines of the Wu family and of Chu Wei but also for her strong support and encouragement, which greatly accelerated my work on this volume. I am grateful for her patience in reading the text and correcting my faulty English during her very busy days in Chungking as Cultural Relations Officer of the American Embassy, in which capacity she has done invaluable work in furthering the cultural relations between the two countries.

Finally, gratitude is due my wife, colleague, and former classmate, Lin Whei-yin (Phyllis), who for more than twenty years has contributed untiringly to our common cause, slaved for me over our architectural school problems (and I slaved for her, too), accompanied me on most of the field trips, made important discoveries, measured and drew a great number of buildings, and has borne with tact and fortitude, in spite of her ill health in recent years, the major share in keeping up the spirit and morale of the Institute throughout the incredibly hard war years. Without her collaboration and inspiration, neither this volume nor any of my work in the study of Chinese architecture would have been possible.★

Liang Ssu-ch'eng
Wartime Station of the
Institute for Research in Chinese Architecture,
Li-chuang, Szechuan
April 1946

★Most of the individuals to whom Liang extended his special thanks in 1946 are deceased. Surviving in addition to myself are Mo Tsung-chiang at Tsing Hua University, Peking, and Shih Chang-ju at Academia Sinica, Taipei.—Ed.

The Chinese Structural System

Origins

The architecture of China is as old as Chinese civilization. From every source of information—literary, graphic, exemplary—there is strong evidence testifying to the fact that the Chinese have always employed an indigenous system of construction that has retained its principal characteristics from prehistoric times to the present day. Over the vast area from Chinese Turkestan to Japan, from Manchuria to the northern half of French Indochina, the same system of construction is prevalent; and this was the area of Chinese cultural influence. That this system of construction could perpetuate itself for more than four thousand years over such a vast territory and still remain a living architecture, retaining its principal characteristics in spite of repeated foreign invasions—military, intellectual, and spiritual—is a phenomenon comparable only to the continuity of the civilization of which it is an integral part.

Near Anyang, Honan Province, at the site of the palaces and necropolis of the Shang–Yin emperors (ca. 1766–ca. 1122 B.C.), excavated by the Academia Sinica, are found the earliest known remains of buildings in China (fig. 10). These are large loess platforms, upon which undressed boulders, flat sides up, are placed at regular intervals, each topped by a bronze disc (later known as a *chih*). On top of these discs are found charred logs, the lower ends of wooden posts that once supported the superstructures that were burned at the sack of the capital when the Yin dynasty fell to the Chou conquerors (ca. 1122 B.C.). The arrangement of these column bases testifies to the existence of a structural system that had by this time taken a definite form and was destined to provide shelter for a great people and their civilization from that time until today.

The basic characteristics of this system, which is still used, consist of a raised platform, forming the base for a structure with a timber post-and-lintel skeleton, which in turn supports a pitched roof with overhanging eaves (figs. 1, 2). This osseous construction permits complete freedom in walling and fenestration and, by the simple adjustment of the proportion between walls and openings, renders a house practical and comfortable in any climate from that of tropical Indochina to that of subarctic Manchuria. Due to its extreme flexibility and adaptability, this method of construction could be employed wherever Chinese civilization spread and would effectively shelter occupants from the elements, however diverse they might be. Perhaps nothing analogous is found in Western architecture, with the limited exception of the Elizabethan half-timber structure in England, until the invention of reinforced concrete and the steel framing systems of the twentieth century.

鴟尾 CH'IH-WEI

脊槫 RIDGE PURLIN

正脊 MAIN RIDGE

垂脊 HIP

平槫 INTERMEDIATE PURLINS

ROOF　屋頂

垂獸 CH'UI-SHOU

平梁 BEAM

柱頭鋪作 SET ON COLUMN

四椽栿 BEAM

撩檐枋或槫 EAVE PURLIN

蹲獸 TSUN-SHOU

補間鋪作 INTERMEDIATE SET

THE STRUCTURAL FRAME　構架

TOU-KUNG　斗栱

轉角鋪作 CORNER SET

COLUMN OR WALL　柱或墙

角柱 CORNER COLUMN

闌額 LINTEL

CENTRAL BAY

平柱 3 COLUMNS

柱礎 BASE

地栿 SILL

壓闌石 CURB

PLATFORM OR STYLOBATE　階基

角柱石 CORNER PIER

隔身版柱 INTERMEDIATE PIERS

踏道 STEPS

NAMES OF PRINCIPAL PARTS OF A CHINESE BUILDING

中國建築主要部份名稱畵

I

Principal parts of a Chinese timber-frame building

LEGEND

1   飛　椽   FEI-CH'UAN, FLYING-RAFTERS
2   檐　椽   YEN-CH'UAN, EAVE-RAFTERS
3   撩檐枋   LIAO-YEN-FANG, EAVE-PURLIN
4   羅漢枋   LO-HAN-FANG, TIE
5   柱頭枋   CHU-T'OU-FANG, TIE
6   井口枋   CHING-K'OU-FANG, TIE
7   襯枋頭   CH'EN-FANG-T'OU
8   散　斗   SHAN-TOU
9   齊心斗   CH'I-SIN-TOU
10 令　拱   LING-KUNG
11 耍　頭   SHUA-T'OU
12 交互斗   CHIAO-HU-TOU
13 慢　拱   MAN-KUNG
14 瓜子拱   KUA-TZŬ-KUNG
15 泥道拱   NI-TAO-KUNG
16 騎栿拱   CH'I-FU-KUNG
17 昂   ANG
17a 昂嘴   BEAK OF THE ANG
18 華頭子   HUA-T'OU-TZŬ
19 華　拱   HUA-KUNG，抄 CH'AO
20 櫨斗   LU-TOU
21 遮椽版   CHÊ-CH'UAN-PAN, RAFTER-HIDING [BOARD
22 檐栿   BEAM
23 闌額   LINTEL OR ARCHITRAVE
24 柱   COLUMN
24a 柱頭   TOP OF COLUMN
25 櫍   CHIH
26 柱礎   BASE
26a 盆唇   P'EN-CH'UN OR LIP
26b 覆盆   FU-P'EN OR PAN
26c 礩   PLINTH

斗拱及全建築之各部均以材（如高中 5.13.17 等）或其分數或倍數為比例之度量單位。自櫨斗出華拱或昂一層謂之一跳，斗拱出跳之數可自一跳至五跳不等本高以三跳（單抄双下昂）為例。

THE PROPORTION OF EACH & ALL PARTS OF A BUILDING IS MEASURED IN TERMS OF THE TS'AI (5, 13, 17, ETC.), ITS MULTIPLES & FRACTION. EACH TIER OF CANTILEVER ARM, EITHER A HUA-KUNG (19) OR AN ANG (17), IS CALLED A T'IAO. A SET OF TOU-KUNG MAY BE MADE UP OF FROM 1 TO 5 T'IAOS. THE EXAMPLE HERE GIVEN IS ONE WITH 3 T'IAOS — 1 HUA-KUNG & 2 ANGS.

CHIH 櫍
BASE 柱礎

中國建築之 "ORDER"·斗拱,檐柱,柱礎   THE CHINESE "ORDER"

2

The Chinese "order" (the most frequently reprinted of Liang's drawings)

Editor's Note: The Curved Roof and Bracket Sets

Figures 1 and 2 present the basic characteristics of traditional Chinese architecture in a way that will be clear to a prepared mind. However, since not every reader will have had the opportunity to see in situ or to study Chinese timber-frame buildings, a few words of further explanation are offered here.

The immediately outstanding feature of Chinese monumental architecture is the curved roof with overhanging eaves, which is supported by a timber skeleton based on a raised platform. Figure 3 illustrates nine variations of the five types of roof construction listed by Liang on page 26. To understand how and why these curved roofs with their upturned eaves are constructed, we must examine the timber skeleton itself. In Liang's words, "the study of the Chinese building is primarily a study of its anatomy. For this reason the section drawings are much more important than the elevations."

3
Five types of roof
1. overhanging gable roof, 2. flush gable roof, 3. hip roof, 4 and 6. gable-and-hip roofs, 5. pyramidal roof, 7–9. double-eaved versions of 5, 6, and 3 respectively.

The section drawings show us that the roof supports in Chinese timber-frame construction differ fundamentally from the conventional Western triangular roof trusses that dictate the rigidity of our straight pitched roofs. The Chinese frame is, instead, markedly flexible (fig. 4). The timber skeleton consists of posts and cross beams rising toward the ridge in diminishing lengths. The purlins—horizontal members that support the rafters—are positioned along the stepped shoulders of the skeleton. The rafters are short, stretching down only from purlin to purlin. By manipulating the heights and widths of the skeleton, a builder can produce a roof of whatever size and curvature are required. The concave curved roof allows the semicylindrical rooftiles to fit together snugly for watertightness.

The extent of eave projection is also remarkable. For example, the eaves of the T'ang temple Fo-kuang Ssu (857 A.D.), which Liang discovered, project about fourteen feet out from their supporting columns (fig. 24). Their importance in sheltering the wooden structure from weather damage for over 1100 years is obvious—for instance, they throw away from the building the rainwater that courses down the tile troughs of the concave roof.

But the immediate function of raising the roof edges is to permit light to penetrate to the interior of the building despite the wide overhang. This necessitates both extending support far outside the interior skeleton to carry the overhanging eave and also building up this support vertically to handle the upturn. How is this achieved?

As Liang points out, "the *tou-kung* [bracket set] plays the leading role, a role so important that no study of Chinese architecture is feasible without a thorough understanding of this element, the governing feature of the Chinese 'order.'" Figure 5 is an isometric view of a bracket set, and figure 6 shows such a *tou-kung* (pronounced doe-goong) in place atop a supporting column. Again we are encountering an exotic element. We in the West are accustomed to simple capitals that receive a direct weight and transfer it to the column. The *tou-kung* is a very complex member. Though its base is simply a large square block on the top of the column, there are set into that block crossed arms (*kung*) spreading in four directions. These in turn bear smaller blocks (*tou*) that carry still longer arms spreading in the four directions to support upper members in balance. The jutting arms (*hua-kung*) rise in tiers or "jumps" and extend outward in steps from the large-block fulcrum to support the weight of the overhanging eaves. This external pressure is countered by internal downthrusts at the other ends of the bracket arms. Intersecting the *hua-kung* in the bracket set are transverse *kung* that parallel the wall plane. Long cantilever arms called *ang* descend from the inner superstructure, balance on the fulcrum, and extend through the bracket sets to support the outermost purlins (fig. 6). This outer burden is countered by the downthrust of upper interior purlins or beams on the "tails" of the *ang*. The extruding "beaks" of the *ang* easily identify them in the bracket sets. Liang explains more fully these and other complexities in the evolution of this construction.—Ed.

ch'a-shou
king post
tiles set on mud
camel hump
liang
short rafter
purlin
t'o-chiao
outside purlins

shua-t'ou
lan-e

4
Section, showing flexible beam skeleton supporting curved roof

5
The basic bracket set

6
Section, showing bracket set and *ang*

tou
hua-kung
transverse kung along the wall line
lu-tou

ang tail

ang beak
lu-tou fulcrum

Two Grammar Books

As this system matured through the ages, a well-regulated set of rules governing design and execution emerged. To study the history of Chinese architecture without a knowledge of these rules is like studying the history of English literature before learning English grammar. Therefore, a brief examination of them is necessary.

For this purpose we are fortunate to have two important books left to us from two epochs of great building activities: the *Ying-tsao fa-shih (Building Standards)* of the Sung dynasty (960–1279) and the *Kung-ch'eng tso-fa tse-li (Structural Regulations)* of the Ch'ing dynasty (1644–1912)—two "grammar books" on Chinese architecture, as we may call them. Both government manuals, they are of the greatest importance for the study of the technological aspects of Chinese architecture. We owe to them all the technical terms that we know and all the criteria that we employ today for the comparative study of the architecture of different periods.

The *Ying-tsao fa-shih*

The *Ying-tsao fa-shih (Building Standards)* was compiled by Li Chieh, superintendent of construction at the court of Emperor Hui-tsung (ruled 1101–1125) of the Sung dynasty. Of the thirty-four chapters thirteen are devoted to rules governing the design of foundations, fortifications, stone masonry and ornamental carving, "major carpentry" (structural framing, columns, beams, lintels, ties, brackets, purlins, rafters, etc.), "minor carpentry" (doors, windows, partitions, screens, ceilings, shrines, etc.), brick and tile masonry (official rank and use of tiles and ornaments), painted decoration (official rank and design of ornamental painting). The rest of the text contains definitions of terms and data for estimation of materials and labor. The last four chapters contain drawings illustrating various kinds of designs in carpentry, stonework, and ornamental painting.

The book was published in 1103. During the eight and a half centuries that have since elapsed, both technical terms and forms have changed, and in an atmosphere in which scholars and literary men looked upon technical and manual work with contempt, the book receded into obscurity and was treasured only by connoisseurs as a rare oddity. It is extremely difficult for the layman today to understand, and many of its passages and terms are almost meaningless. Due to the conscientious efforts of the Institute for Research in Chinese Architecture, first by mastery of the regulations of the Ch'ing dynasty (the *Kung-ch'eng tso-fa tse-li*), and later with the discovery of a considerable number of wooden structures dating from the tenth to the twelfth centuries, many mysteries of the book have been clarified, rendering it now quite "readable."

Because timber is the principal material used in Chinese architecture, the chapters on "major carpentry" are the most important part of the book for understanding the structural system. The essentials of these rules are explained visually in figures 2 and 7 and may be summed up as follows.

1. Modules (*ts'ai* and *ch'i*)

The term *ts'ai* has a twofold meaning:

(a) A standard-sized timber used for the *kung*, or "arms" of a set of brackets (*tou-kung*); and all timbers of the same depth and width. There are eight sizes, or grades, of *ts'ai*, which are determined by the type and official rank of the building to be erected.

(b) A module for measurement, described as follows:

The depth of each *ts'ai* is to be divided into 15 equal parts, called *fen*, and the width of the *ts'ai* is to be ten *fen*. The height and breadth of every building, the dimensions of every member in the structure, the rise and curve of the roofline, in short, every measurement in the building, is to be measured in terms of *fen* of the grade of *ts'ai* used.

When two *ts'ai* are used one above another, it is customary to cushion them by filling the gap with a block six *fen* in height, called a *ch'i*. A member measuring one *ts'ai* and one *ch'i* in depth is called a *tsu-ts'ai*, or "full *ts'ai*." The measurements of, and the proportions between the different parts of a building of the Sung dynasty are always expressed in terms of the *ts'ai*, *ch'i*, and *fen* of the grade of *ts'ai* used.

2. Bracket Sets (*tou-kung*)

A set of *tou-kung*, or brackets, is an assemblage of a number of *tou* (blocks) and *kung* (arms). The function of the set is to transfer the load from the horizontal member above to the vertical member below. A set may be placed either on the column, or on the architrave between two columns, or on the corner column. Accordingly, a set of *tou-kung* may be called a "column set," "intermediate set," or "corner set" depending on the position it occupies. The members that make up a set may be divided into three main categories: *tou*, *kung*, and *ang*. There are four kinds of *tou* and five kinds of *kung*, determined by their functions and positions. But structurally the most important members of a set are the *lu-tou*, or major bearing block, and the *hua-kung*, or arms extending out from it to form cantilevers to both front and rear, at right angles to the facade of the building. Sometimes a slanting member, at approximately a 30-degree angle to the ground, is placed above the *hua-kung*; it is called the *ang*. The "tail" or upper end of the *ang* is often held down by the weight of the beam or the purlin, making it a lever arm for the support of the large overhang of the eave.

The *hua-kung* may be used in successive tiers, each extending front and rear a certain distance beyond the tier below. Such a tier and extension is called a *t'iao*, or "jump," and the number of *t'iao* in a set may vary from one to five. Transverse *kung* intersect the *hua-kung* in the *lu-tou*. One or two tiers of transverse *kung* may be used in a *t'iao*. Such an arrangement is known as *chi-hsin*, or "accounted heart," while a *t'iao* without transverse *kung* is known as *t'ou-hsin*, or "stolen heart." One tier of transverse *kung* is called *tan-kung*, or single *kung*; a double tier is called *ch'ung-kung*, or double *kung*. By varying the number of "jumps," by "accounting" or "stealing" the "hearts," by cantilevering with *hua-kung* or with *ang*, and by using single or double transverse *kung*, different combinations of the *tou-kung* can be assembled.

7

Sung dynasty rules for structural carpentry

3. Beams

The size and shape of a beam varies according to its function and position. The beams below a ceiling are called *ming-fu*, or "exposed beams." They are either straight or slightly arched; the latter is called *yüeh-liang*, or "crescent-moon beam." Above the ceiling *ts'ao-fu*, or "rough beams," are used to receive the load of the roof. The circumference of a beam may vary according to its length, but the cross section always retains, as a norm, a ratio of 3 : 2 between its depth and width.

4. Columns

Rules governing the length and the diameter of a column are rather loose. The diameter may vary from one *ts'ai*-plus-one *ch'i* to three *ts'ai*. The column may be either straight or shuttle-shaped. The latter is given an entasis on the upper third of the shaft. The most important rules in columniation are: (1) a gradual increase in the height of the columns from the central bay toward the corners of the building, and (2) a slight inward incline of the columns, about 1 : 100. These refinements help give an illusion of stability.

5. The Curved Roof (*chü-che*)

The profile of the roof plane is determined by means of a *chü*, or "raising" of the ridge purlin, and a *che*, or "depression" of the rafter line. The pitch is determined by the "raise" of the ridge, which may make a slope varying from 1 : 2 for a small house to 2 : 3 for a large hall, with gradations in between. The height of the raise is called the *chü-kao*. The curve of the rafter line is obtained by "depressing" or lowering the position of the first purlin below the ridge, by one-tenth of the height of the *chü-kao*, off a straight line from the ridge to the eave purlin. Another straight line is then drawn from this newly plotted point to the eave purlin, and the next purlin below is "depressed" by one-twentieth of the *chü-kao*. The process is repeated, and each time the "depression" is reduced by half. The points thus obtained are joined by a series of straight lines and the roof line is plotted. This process is called *che-wu*, or "bending the roof."

Besides these basic rules, Sung methods for the use and shaping of architraves, ties, hip rafters, purlins, common rafters, and other elements are carefully specified in the *Ying-tsao fa-shih*. A careful study of the evolution of the major carpentry of different periods introduced in later chapters gives a fairly clear idea of the development of the Chinese structural system through the ages.

The chapters on minor carpentry give rules for the designing of doors, windows, partitions, screens, and other nonstructural elements. The tradition is generally carried on in later ages without drastic modification. Ceiling coffers are either square or rectangular, and the large principal coffer is often decorated with miniature *tou-kung*. Even Buddhist and Taoist shrines are highly architectural in character and are decorated with *tou-kung*.

The chapter on tile and tile ornaments specifies the sizes and numbers of the ornamental dragon heads and "sitting beasts" that decorate the ridges, according to the official rank and size of the building. The making of a ridge by piling up ordinary roof tiles, though still practiced today in southern China, is a method no longer used in monumental architecture.

The chapters on decorative painting specify the kinds of painting for different ranks of buildings. Rules also govern the distribution of colors, mainly on the principle of contrasting warm and cool colors. We also learn that the shading of colors is obtained by the juxtaposition of colors related in the chromatic scale rather than by deepening a single color. The principal colors used are blue, red, and green, accented with black and white. Yellow is occasionally used. This tradition has been followed from the T'ang dynasty (618–907) to the present.

A great deal of attention is also paid to the details of parts and members, such as the shaping and curving of the *tou*, *kung*, and *ang*, the arching of the beam and the pulvination of its sides, the carving of ornaments on pedestals and balustrades, and the color schemes of various types and grades of decorative painting. In many respects the *Ying-tsao fa-shih* is a textbook in the modern sense of the word.

The *Kung-ch'eng tso-fa tse-li*

The *Kung-ch'eng tso-fa tse-li (Structural Regulations)* was published in 1734 by the Ministry of Construction of the Ch'ing dynasty. The first twenty-seven chapters are rules for constructing twenty-seven kinds of buildings, such as halls, city gates, residences, barns, and pavilions. The size of each structural member in each building type is carefully specified, differentiating this book from the *Ying-tsao fa-shih*, which gives general rules and ratios for designing and computation. The next thirteen chapters specify the dimensions of each kind of *tou-kung* and the sequence of assembling them. Seven chapters treat doors, windows, partitions, screens, and stone, brick, and earth masonry. The last twenty-four chapters are rules for the estimation of materials and labor.

The only drawings are twenty-seven cross sections of the twenty-seven building types described. There are no instructions for details, such as the shaping of the *kung* and *ang*, decorative paintings, and the like, which would have been permeated with the characteristics of the time. This drawback, however, is fortunately overcome by the existence of numerous examples of Ch'ing dynasty architecture that can be conveniently studied.

From the first forty-seven chapters of the *Kung-ch'eng tso-fa tse-li* a number of principles can be derived, of which the following, explained visually in figure 8, are the most important ones concerning major carpentry or structural design.

1. Reduction in the Depth of the *Ts'ai*

As noted above, the depth of the *ts'ai* of the Sung style is 15 *fen* (with a width of ten *fen*) and the *ch'i* measures six *fen*, resulting in a *tsu-ts'ai*, or "full *ts'ai*," of 21 *fen* in depth. However, the concept of *ts'ai*, *ch'i*, and *fen* does not seem to have existed in the minds of the builders of the Ch'ing dynasty. The *tou-k'ou*, or "mortise of the *tou*" [literally "block mouth"], for receiving the *kung* is specified as the Ch'ing module. It is equivalent to the

RULES FOR STRUCTURAL CARPENTRY ACCORDING TO KUNG-CH'ENG-TSO-FA

清工程做法則例
雍正十二年工部頒布刊行
大式大木
畫樣要略

OFFICIAL REGULATIONS FOR ARCHITECTURAL DESIGN IN THE CH'ING DYNASTY, PUBLISHED BY THE MINISTRY OF WORKS IN 1733.

柱間距離以十一斗口之倍數定
INTERCOLUMN DISTANCES DETERMINED BY MULTIPLES OF 11 TOU-K'OU

明間用平身科六攢或八攢
6 OR 8 INTERMEDIATE SETS FOR CENTRAL BAY

柱頭科 SET ON COLUMN

平身科 INTERMEDIATE SETS

角科 CORNER SET

雀替 BRACKET

盡間　梢間　次間　明間

梁 按柱徑加二寸定梁厚,以厚之五分之六定高。斷面高與厚成6:5或5:4之比。
WIDTH OF BEAM = DIAMETER OF COLUMN + 2 INCHES; DEPTH = 6/5 WIDTH. THUS RATIO BETWEEN DEPTH & WIDTH OF BEAM IS AROUND 6:5 OR 5:4.

柱 凡檐柱,以6斗口定徑,以60斗口定高。其他部位之柱,據檐柱加舉定高,徑視檐柱徑增二寸為定法。不側腳,無卷殺。唯收分7/1000。 PERIPTERAL COLUMN IS 6 TOU-K'OU IN DIAMETER, 60 TOU-K'OU IN HEIGHT. DIAMETER FOR HYPOSTYLE COLUMN = 6 TOU-K'OU + 2 INCHES.

HEIGHT OF COLUMN 柱高 = 60斗口 TOU-K'OU = 10 DIAMETER

攢 斗拱一組也,宋稱朵。攢與攢間之距離定為十一斗口,開間面濶以攢數定之。
A SET OF TOU-KUNG IS CALLED A TSAN. SETS ARE SPACED AT INTERVALS OF 11 TOU-K'OU, MULTIPLES OF WHICH GIVES WIDTHS OF BAYS.

攢中　攢中　攢中
11斗口　11斗口　11斗口

鼓鏡 KU-CHING "MIRROR BASE"

6斗口

舉架 CHÜ-CHIA OR "RAISING THE TRUSS"
自下向上,每一搭之坡度遞加,最下架坡度為50%坡,次70%,次80%,最上90%加平水,即所謂五舉七舉八舉九舉者是也。故脊之高非預定者,乃由下向上遞加所得也。
THE PITCH OF EACH SECTION OF THE RAFTER IS INCREASED FROM THE EAVE UP TOWARDS THE RIDGE. THE LOWEST SECTION IS A 50% SLOPE; THE NEXT, 70%; THE NEXT, 80%; TO THE 90% RAISE OF THE TOP SECTION IS ADDED A "PING-SHUI" OF 4 TOU-K'OU, MAKING APPROXIMATELY A 100% OR 45° SLOPE.

步架 X　步架 X　步架 X　步架 X

平水 P'ING-SHUI 4斗口

三架梁 3-PURLIN BEAM

五架梁 5-PURLIN BEAM

七架梁 7-PURLIN BEAM

金柱 HYPOSTYLE COLUMN

桃尖梁

平板枋 PLATE

闌額 LINTEL

由額 SUB-LINTEL

檐柱 PERISTYE COLUMN

拱 KUNG
昂 ANG
拱 KUNG
斗 TOU

斗拱 TOU-KUNG
在比例上小於宋式甚多。用材以足材為主,各魯枋間均不用斗。PROPORTIONALLY MUCH SMALLER THAN SUNG TOU-KUNG. TOU NO LONGER USED BETWEEN HORIZONTAL TIE MEMBERS.

斗口 TOU-K'OU 清式稱材厚曰斗口,即宋之十分也。斗口自一寸至六寸,共十一等,但實物所見,最大者僅至四寸。用材均高二斗口,單材僅用枚跳頭橫拱,高為1.4斗口。 THE WIDTH OF A TS'AI IS KNOWN AS A TOU-K'OU, RANGING FROM 1 TO 6 INCHES; DEPTH OF TS'AI = 2 TOU-K'OU. TAN-TS'AI, OR A LIGHT TS'AI = 2 × 1.4 TOU-K'OU, USED ONLY FOR KUNGS EMPLOYED ON T'IAOS.

斗口 TOU-K'OU
斗口　斗口

width of the *kung*, and therefore, of the *ts'ai* (ten *fen* in terms of Sung construction). The dimensions and proportions of the parts of a *tou-kung* bracket are now expressed in multiples or fractions of the *tou-k'ou*. While retaining the six *fen* (now 0.6 *tou-k'ou*) for the gap between the upper and lower *kung*, the depth of the *kung*, or *ts'ai*, itself is reduced from 15 to 14 *fen* (now 1.4 *tou-k'ou*). The *tsu-ts'ai* is then reduced to only 20 *fen*, or two *tou-k'ou* in depth.

There is another major difference between Sung and Ch'ing bracket sets. In the Sung period the major block (*lu-tou*), in which the cross arms rest on the center line of columns parallel to the facade, supports several tiers of *ts'ai* with open or plaster-filled gaps between. These tiers are cushioned by *tou* blocks. In the Ch'ing set the tiers of *tsu-ts'ai*, measuring one × two *tou-k'ou*, are laid one directly on top of another. Thus the *ch'i*, or gaps allowing space for the *tou*, are eliminated. These seemingly trifling modifications affect the general aspect of the *tou-kung* so much that the difference is immediately apparent by even a casual glance.

2. A Specific Ratio between the Diameter and the Height of the Column

The Ch'ing regulations specify the diameter of a column as six *tou-k'ou* (four *ts'ai* in Sung terms), and its height as 60 *tou-k'ou* or ten diameters. The diameter of a column of the Sung dynasty, according to the *Ying-tsao fa-shih*, never exceeded three *ts'ai*, and the height was left to the discretion of the designer. Thus proportionally the Ch'ing column is much enlarged and the *tou-kung* drastically reduced in size, dwindling into insignificant pettiness. An unprecedented increase in the number of intermediate bracket sets results. In some cases seven or eight intermediate sets are perched on the architrave between two columns; in the Sung dynasty the number never exceeded two, both according to the *Ying-tsao fa-shih* and as evidenced in existing buildings.

3. The Length and Width of a Building Determined by the Number of *Tou-kung*

As the number of intermediate sets is increased, the distance between them is strictly specified as 11 *tou-k'ou* center to center. Consequently the distances between columns, and therefore the length and width of a building, must necessarily be determined by multiples of 11 *tou-k'ou*.

4. All Facade Columns of Equal Height

The Sung practice of increasing the height of the columns toward the corners of the building was discontinued. The columns, though slightly tapered, are straight with no entasis. Thus a Ch'ing building as a whole presents a more rigid appearance than a Sung structure. The slight inward incline, however, is still the rule.

5. Increase in the Width of the Beams

Beams of the Sung dynasty generally have a ratio of 3 : 2 between their depth and width. In the Ch'ing rules the ratio is changed to 5 : 4 or 6 : 5, betraying an obvious ignorance of mechanics and of the strength of materials. Moreover, the overall rule of making the beam "two inches [*fen*] wider than the diameter of the column" seems most arbitrary and irrational. All beams are straight; the "crescent-moon beam" has no place in official Ch'ing architecture.

6. Steeper Pitch of the Curved Roof

What is called in the Sung dynasty *chü-che* ("raise–depress") is known in the Ch'ing dynasty as *chü-chia*, or "raising the frame." The two methods, though bringing about more or less similar results, are entirely different in their basic conceptions. The height of the ridge purlin of the Sung structure is predetermined, and the curvature of the roofline is achieved by "depressing" the successive purlins below. The Ch'ing builder starts from the bottom, giving the first *pu* or "step" (that is, the distance between the two lowest purlins) a "five *chü*," or a pitch of 5 : 10; the second step a "six *chü*," or 6 : 10; the third, $6\frac{1}{2}$: 10; the fourth, $7\frac{1}{2}$: 10; and up to "nine *chü*," or 9 : 10. The position of the ridge purlin becomes the incidental outcome of the successive steps. The pitch of the Ch'ing roof thus obtained is generally steeper than that of the Sung roof, giving a convenient clue for identifying and dating.

As we shall see below, a Ch'ing building is generally characterized by harshness and rigidity in the lines of the posts and lintels, in the excessively steep pitch of the roof, and in the smallness of the *tou-kung* under the eave. Perhaps it was the uncompromising strictness of the dimensions given in the *Kung-ch'eng tso-fa tse-li* that succeeded in effacing all the suavity and elegance that we find so charming in a building from the period of the *Ying-tsao fa-shih*.

Neither book mentions ground plans. The *Ying-tsao fa-shih* contains a few plans, but they show columniation, not the internal division of spaces. Unlike European buildings, the Chinese building, whether house or temple, is rarely planned by subdividing the individual unit. Since it may be subdivided so easily by means of wooden partitions or screens between any two columns, the problem of internal planning hardly exists. Planning, instead, concerns the external grouping of individual units. The general principle is the arrangement of buildings around a courtyard, or rather an arrangement that forms a courtyard or patio. The buildings are sometimes connected by colonnades, but these are eliminated in smaller houses. A large house is composed of a series of courtyards along a common axis, and deviation from this principle is rare. The same principle is applied to both religious and secular architecture. In plan there is no basic difference between a temple and a residence. Thus it was not an uncommon practice in ancient times for a high official, or even a rich merchant, to donate his residence to the service of Buddha and have it consecrated as a temple.

Pre-Buddhist and Cave-Temple Evidence of Timber-Frame Architecture

Indirect Material Evidence

The Shang–Yin remains near Anyang mentioned in the previous chapter are merely ruins (fig. 10). It is by inference that we come to the conclusion that the Chinese structural system was basically the same then as today. For proof we have to turn to examples from later periods.

The earliest source that reveals the appearance of a timber-frame building is the relief on a bronze vase of the period of the Warring States (403–221 B.C.) of the Chou dynasty (fig. 9). It shows on a platform a two-storied building with columns, eaved roofs, doors, and railings. From a structural point of view, this building must have had a plan essentially the same as the remains at the Shang–Yin site. Particularly significant are the indications of columns with the characteristic bracket sets, or *tou-kung*, which were later formulated into strict proportions very much like the orders in European architecture. Aside from this specimen and the Anyang remains, and perhaps a few other rather insignificant and inadequate representations on bronzes and lacquers, architecture before the Christian era in China is veiled in obscurity. It is highly doubtful that future archaeological excavations will be able to shed much light on the appearance of the superstructure of Chinese buildings in a period of such remote antiquity.

9
Early pictorial representation of a Chinese house

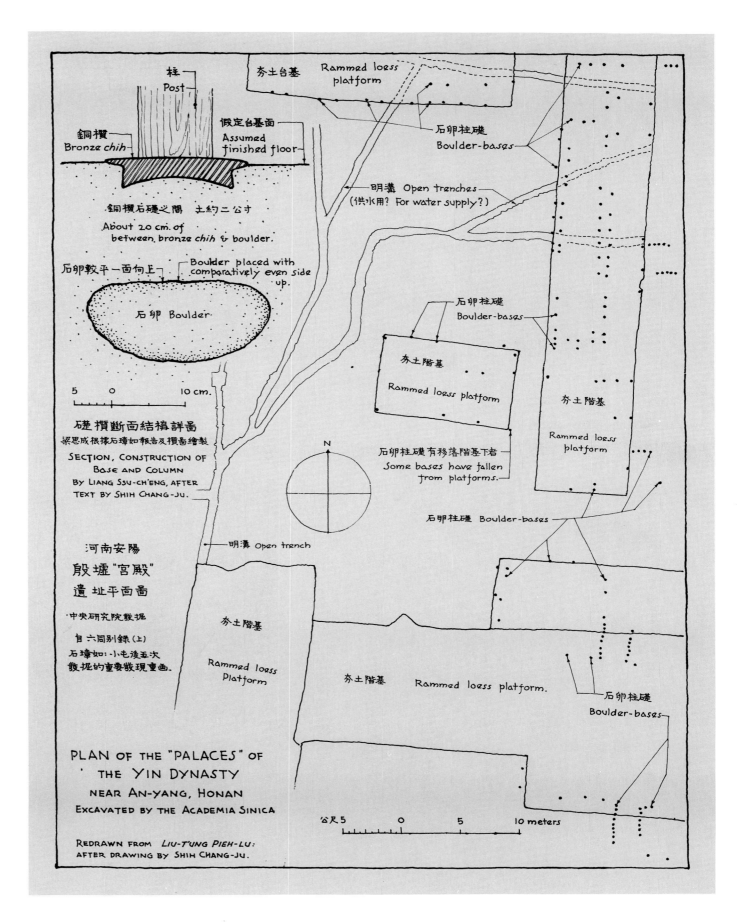

柱
Post

銅櫍
Bronze *chih*

假定台基面
Assumed finished floor

夯土台基
Rammed loess platform

石卵柱礎
Boulder-bases

銅櫍石礎之間　土約二公寸
About 20 cm. of between. bronze *chih* & boulder.

石卵較平一面向上
Boulder placed with comparatively even side up.

石卵 Boulder

明溝 Open trenches
(供水用? For water supply?)

5　0　　10 cm.

礎櫍斷面結構詳圖
梁思成根據石璋如報告及櫍圖繪製
SECTION, CONSTRUCTION OF BASE AND COLUMN
BY LIANG SSU-CH'ENG, AFTER TEXT BY SHIH CHANG-JU.

河南安陽
殷墟"宮殿"
遺址平面圖

中央研究院發掘

自 六同別錄（上）
石璋如：小屯後五次
發掘的重要發現畫畫。

N

石卵柱礎
Boulder-bases

夯土階基
Rammed loess platform

夯土階基
Rammed loess platform

石卵柱礎有移落階基下者
Some bases have fallen from platforms.

明溝 Open trench

石卵柱礎　Boulder-bases

夯土階基
Rammed loess Platform

夯土階基　Rammed loess platform.

石卵柱礎
Boulder-bases

PLAN OF THE "PALACES" OF
THE YIN DYNASTY
NEAR AN-YANG, HONAN
EXCAVATED BY THE ACADEMIA SINICA

公尺 5　　0　　5　　10 meters

REDRAWN FROM *LIU-T'UNG PIEH-LU*:
AFTER DRAWING BY SHIH CHANG-JU.

Han Evidence

The earliest remains of real architectural importance are to be found in the tombs of the Eastern Han dynasty (25–220 A.D.). These monuments may be classified into three categories: (1) rock-cut tombs (fig. 11), some highly architectural, mostly in Szechuan Province and a small number in Hunan Province; (2) freestanding pylonlike monuments, called *ch'üeh* (fig. 12), usually in pairs, flanking the entrance to the avenue leading to a palace, temple, or tomb; (3) small shrines in the form of houses (fig. 13), usually placed in front of the tumulus of a tomb. All these relics are of stone, but the essentials of the *tou-kung* and the trabeated construction are so faithfully represented that a fairly clear idea of the wooden structures after which these monuments are modeled can be gathered from them.

Salient characteristics of the architecture of this period, as seen in these three kinds of remains, are: (1) the octagonal column, capped by a very large *tou* or block that often shows a filletlike molding at its bottom, representing the *ming-pan*, a square, small board;★ (2) the *kung* arm with an S-curve, which seems unlikely and therefore may not have been the actual way of shaping timbers at that time; (3) roof and eaves supported by rafters and covered by tubular tiles with ridge ornaments.

Of the wooden palaces and houses of the Han dynasty, whose magnificence we can now know only from contemporary odes and essays, there is not a single standing example. But from clay models of houses buried in tombs (fig. 14) and from reliefs decorating the walls of the tomb shrines (fig. 15), it is not difficult to form an idea of Han domestic architecture. There are both multistoried mansions and modest houses of the common people. There is one example of an L-shaped elevation, with a walled court-yard in the angle of the L. (fig. 16). We even detect in a watch tower the forerunner of the Buddhist pagoda. The timber-frame system of construction is clearly represented in some of the models. Here again the *tou-kung* plays the leading role, a role so important that no study of Chinese architecture is feasible without a thorough understanding of this element, the governing feature of the Chinese "order." We also find all five kinds of roof construction used in later ages: the hip roof, the flush gable roof, the overhanging gable roof, the gable and hip roof, and the pyramidal roof (fig. 3). The use of the tubular tile was evidently already as common as it is today.

★This element disappeared from Chinese architecture after the sixth or seventh century. The term *ming-pan* is borrowed from the Japanese term designating the element in Japanese architecture of the seventh and eighth centuries. —Ed.

11
Han rock-cut tombs near
Chiang-k'ou, Peng-shan,
Szechuan
a
Plans and details
b
A tomb

12
Han stone *ch'üeh*. These piers imitate contemporary simple wood construction.

13
Han free–standing tomb shrines

14
Clay house models from Han
tombs

力神
'Caryatid'

力神
'Caryatid'

斗栱
Tou-kung

柱礎
Base

臨水亭榭 (其一)
两城山画象石
WATER-FRONT PAVILION
FROM LIANG-CH'ENG SHAN

重樓
武氏祠画象石
TWO-STOREYED BUILDING
FROM THE WU FAMILY SHRINES

三跳斗栱
3-tier-
tou-kung

兩跳斗栱
2-tier-
tou-kung

平坐斗栱
P'ing-tso sets

臨水亭榭 (其二)
WATER-FRONT PAVILION
FROM LIANG-CH'ENG SHAN

重樓 並 雙闕 TWO-STOREYED BUILDING WITH CH'ÜEH
紐約博物館藏石 (METROPOLITON MUSEUM, NEW YORK.)

斗栱 Tou-kung

橋
武氏祠画象石
BRIDGE
FROM THE WU FAMILY SHRINES

鎭管 Door knockers

城門 咸 (函) 谷關東門畵象
CITY-GATE
EAST GATE OF HAN-KU KUAN
(BOSTON MUSEUM OF FINE ARTS)

漢画象石中 ARCHITECTURE FOUND IN ENGRAVED STONES
建築數種 (OR RELIEFS) OF THE HAN DYNASTY 205 B.C.-220 A.D.

15
Architecture depicted in Han engraved reliefs

16
Han funerary clay house model, Nelson–Atkins Museum, Kansas City, Missouri. The structural frame of a three-story Han dwelling is indicated by crude modeling and painting. *Tou-kung* are used not only under the eaves but also under the balcony. Corner bracket sets are introduced on the third story, but the solution is not satisfactory. The two corner towers flanking the gate are similar to the stone *ch'üeh* found in North China.

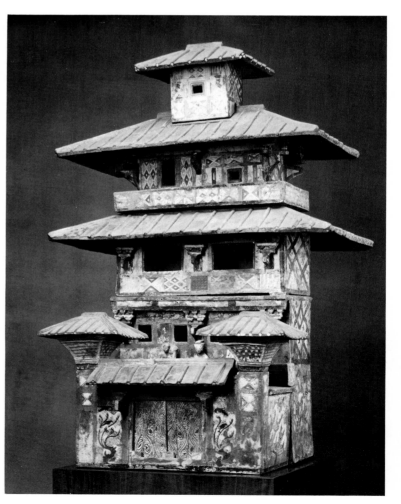

Buddhism reached China at approximately the beginning of the Christian era. Though there are records of the erection of a Buddhist pagoda as early as the beginning of the third century A.D., described as "a multi-storied tower surmounted by a pile of metal discs," we possess today no Buddhist monument before the middle of the fifth century. However, from then on until the later fourteenth century, the history of Chinese architecture is chiefly the history of Buddhist (and a few Taoist) temples and their pagodas.

The Caves of Yun-kang (450–500 A.D.), near Ta-t'ung, Shansi Province, though unquestionably Indian in origin, with prototypes in Karli, Ajanta, and elsewhere in India, show surprisingly little influence from their land of origin. The architectural treatment of the caves is almost exclusively Chinese. The only indications of foreign influence are the idea of the cave temple itself and the Greco–Buddhist motifs in the ornaments, such as the acanthus leaf, the egg-and-dart, the swastika, the garland, the bead, and others, which have enriched and become a part of the vocabulary of Chinese ornamental motifs (fig. 17).

The architecture of the Yun-kang Caves may be studied from two points of view: (1) the caves themselves, including the architectural treatment of the exteriors and interiors, and (2) contemporary wooden and masonry architecture represented in the reliefs decorating the cave walls (fig. 18). Among these depictions are numerous halls and pagodas, structures that once rose in great numbers all over the plains and hills of northern and central China.

The hewing out of cave temples from rocky cliffs was practiced in the north until the middle of the T'ang dynasty (618–907), and carried on thereafter in the southwest, notably in Szechuan Province, until the Ming dynasty (1368–1644). Only the earlier cave temples are of interest to the architectural historian. The apogee of their architectural quality was reached in the caves of the Northern Ch'i and Sui dynasties (late sixth and early seventh centuries) at T'ien-lung Shan, near T'ai-yuan, Shansi Province, and at Hsiang-t'ang Shan, on the border of the provinces of Honan and Hopei (fig. 19).

These caves have preserved in stone faithful copies of the wooden architecture of their time. We notice among the salient characteristics that the columns in most cases are octagonal, with capitals in the shape of a *lu-tou*, similar to those found in the rock-cut tombs of the Han dynasty. Above the capitals is placed the architrave, which, in turn, is to receive the *lu-tou* of the set of *tou-kung*. This arrangement was in later ages modified by mortising the architrave directly onto the upper end of the column, and (combining the two *lu-tou* into one) placing the *lu-tou* of the bracket set directly on the column.

In the treatment of these caves, the *tou-kung* is always the dominant architectural feature. It is still simple, as in the Han dynasty, but the S-curve of the *kung* has by now straightened into a more plausible form. An intermediate set, in the form of an inverted letter V, is introduced on the architrave spanning the two columns. Because it resembles the Chinese character for man (*jen*), it is sometimes dubbed *jen-tzu kung*, "man-character arm." With the exception of one surviving specimen, the Tomb Pagoda of Ching-tsang (746) in the Sung Mountains, Honan Province (figs. 64d, e), where this feature is represented in brick, it is now preserved in only a few contemporary wooden structures in Japan.

17
Detail of an interior doorway,
Yun-kang Caves, near
Ta-t'ung, Shansi, 450–500

18
Architectural elements carved
in the Yun-kang Caves

大門 GATE WAY

木塔 WOODEN T'A (PAGODA)

中部第八洞東壁浮彫佛殿
THREE-BAYED TEMPLE HALL

木塔 WOODEN PAGODA

中部第八洞獸形斗拱
DOUBLE-LION TOU-KUNG
PERSIAN INFLUENCE

中部第八洞
伊阿尼式柱
"IONIC" CAPITAL
GREEK INFLUENCE

藻井四種 CAISSON CEILINGS

ARCHITECTURE IN THE
YÜN-KANG CAVES, TA-TUNG,
SHANSI, WEI DYNASTY
EXECUTED BETWEEN 450 & 500 A.D.

雲岡石窟所表現之北魏建築

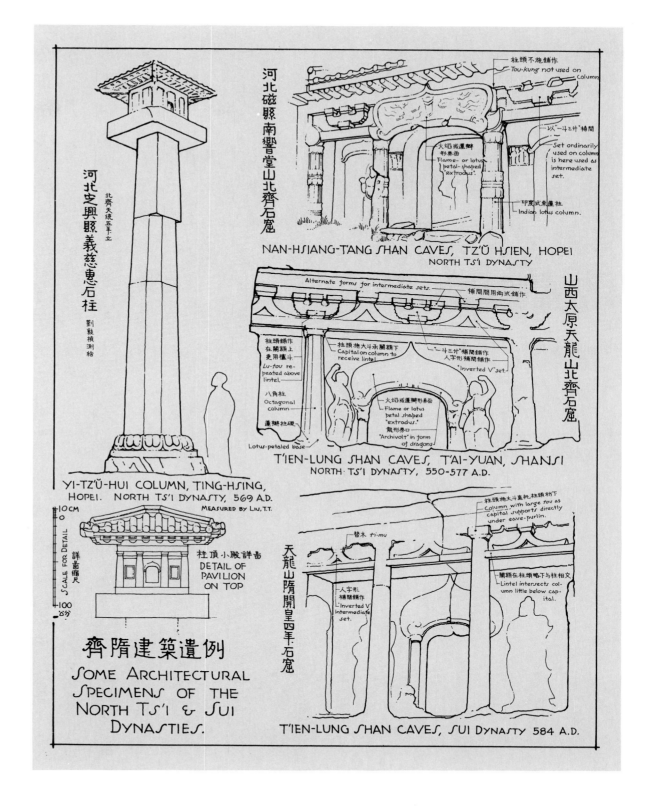

河北磁縣南響堂山北齊石窟

NAN-HSIANG-TANG SHAN CAVES, TZ'Ŭ HSIEN, HOPEI
NORTH TS'I DYNASTY

山西太原天龍山北齊石窟

T'IEN-LUNG SHAN CAVES, T'AI-YUAN, SHANSI
NORTH·TS'I DYNASTY, 550-577 A.D.

河北定興縣義慈惠石柱

北齊天統五年立

劉敦楨測繪

YI-TZ'Ŭ-HUI COLUMN, TING-HSING,
HOPEI. NORTH TS'I DYNASTY, 569 A.D.
MEASURED BY LIU, T.T.

DETAIL OF
PAVILION
ON TOP

柱頂小殿詳畫

詳畫瘤尺
SCALE FOR DETAIL

齊隋建築遺例
SOME ARCHITECTURAL
SPECIMENS OF THE
NORTH TS'I & SUI
DYNASTIES.

天龍山隋開皇四年石窟

T'IEN-LUNG SHAN CAVES, SUI DYNASTY 584 A.D.

Timber, which is the principal building material employed by the Chinese, is highly perishable, subject to natural decay from the elements and from pests. It is highly flammable and, when used for a religious building, is constantly exposed to the danger of fire from the incense and candles of the worshippers. Moreover, a land periodically razed by civil wars and religious struggles proved none too favorable for the conservation of timber structures. The customary sack of the capital of the vanquished by the founder of a new dynasty, who was usually either a rebel, a warlord, or a leader of a less developed nation from the north, usually with great animosity toward the defeated ruler, has deprived posterity of every trace of the glory and splendor of every single palace of numberless princes, kings, and emperors. (Among the very few notable exceptions to this barbarous custom was the founding of the Republic in 1912: the palaces of the Ch'ing emperors were opened to the public as a museum.)

Although China has always been considered a land of freedom of worship, there were at least three great persecutions of Buddhism from the fifth to the ninth centuries. The last of these outrages occurred in 845 and almost stripped the country of all Buddhist temples and monasteries. These practices, and the highly perishable nature of the material, probably account for the total absence of timber structures before the middle of the ninth century.

Recent tendencies in China, especially since the founding of the Republic, have not been favorable for the preservation of ancient edifices. After repeated defeats by the modern powers from the middle of the nineteenth century, the Chinese intellectual and governing class lost confidence in everything of its own. Its standard of beauty was totally confused: the old was thrown away; of the new, or Western, it was ignorant. Buddhism and Taoism were condemned as sheer superstition and, not unjustly, as among the causes for the sluggishness of the people. The general tendency was iconoclastic. A great many temples were confiscated and secularized, and were utilized by antitraditional officials as schools, offices, grain storages, or even as barracks, ammunition dumps, and asylums. At best the buildings were remodeled to suit the new functions, while at worst the unfortunate structures were put at the disposal of ill-disciplined and underpaid soldiers, who, for lack of proper fuel, tore down every removable part—partitions, doors, windows, railings, and even *tou-kung*—for the cooking of their meals.

It was not until late in the twenties that Chinese intellectuals began to realize the significance of their own architecture as an art no less important than calligraphy and painting. First, a number of buildings appeared, built by foreigners but in the Chinese style. Next, Western and Japanese scholars published books and articles on Chinese architecture. And, finally, a number of Chinese students who had gone abroad to study Western techniques of building came back with the realization that architecture is something more than brick and timber: it is an art, an expression of the people and their times, and a cultural heritage. The contempt of the educated class for matters of "masonry and carpentry" gradually turned into appreciation and admiration. But it was a long time before this consciousness could be implanted in the minds of the local authorities upon whom the protection of antiquities depends. Meanwhile the process of deterioration and destruction steadily progressed in the hands of the ignorant and the negligent.

Finally, the destruction brought about by the war of Japanese aggression (1937–1945) is still unknown. It should be no surprise to find that many of the monuments recorded in this volume will hereafter be known only by these photographs and drawings.

Wooden structures existing today, or rather known to have existed when they were last seen in the 1930s, may be tentatively divided into three main periods: the Period of Vigor, the Period of Elegance, and the Period of Rigidity (figs. 20, 21).

The Period of Vigor includes the phase from the middle of the ninth century to the middle of the eleventh century, or from the reign of Emperor Hsuan-tsung of the T'ang dynasty to the end of the reign of Emperor Jen-tsung of the Sung dynasty. This period is characterized by a robustness of proportion and construction which must have been that of the glorious T'ang dynasty and of which this is but its magnificent conclusion.

The Period of Elegance extended from the middle of the eleventh century to the end of the fourteenth century or from the reign of Emperor Ying-tsung of the Sung dynasty, through the Yuan dynasty, to the death of Emperor T'ai-tsu, founder of the Ming dynasty. It is marked by a gracefulness in proportion and refinement in detail.

The Period of Rigidity lasted from the beginning of the fifteenth century to the end of the nineteenth century, or from the reign of Emperor Ch'eng-tsu (Yung-lo) of the Ming dynasty, who usurped his nephew's throne and moved the capital from Nanking to Peking, to the overthrow of the Ch'ing dynasty by the Republic. It is identified by a general rigidity, a clumsiness of proportion resulting from the excessive size of all horizontal members, and the decrease in size (in proportion to the building) of the *tou-kung*, hence the increase in number of the intermediate sets, which have by this time degenerated from their original structural function to mere ornaments.

This division of periods is, of course, fairly arbitrary. It is impossible to draw a line of demarcation to separate the imperceptible steps in the process of evolution. Thus a building of an early date may be found heralding a new style or feature, or in regions far from the cultural and political centers, a late structure may tenaciously cling to a bygone tradition. A generous margin must be allowed for the overlapping of the periods.

21

Comparison of plan and
columniation of timber–frame
halls

The Period of Vigor (ca. 850–1050)

Indirect Material Evidence

The Period of Vigor—only a few specimens of its final phase remain—must have had a brilliant past stretching considerably before the middle of the ninth century, perhaps as far back as the beginning of the T'ang dynasty, or early seventh century. As to the wooden buildings of this hypothetical first half of the period, we can only resort to contemporary graphic art for information. An incised relief on the tympanum over the west doorway of the Ta-yen T'a or Wild Goose Pagoda (701–704) in Sian, Shensi Province (fig. 22), depicts in detail and with great accuracy the main hall of a Buddhist temple. It shows for the first time the brackets with outstretching arms, or *hua-kung*, used as cantilevers to support the great overhang of the eave. This does not imply that the *hua-kung* was not used previously; on the contrary, it must have been in use for quite a long time, perhaps even a few hundred years, before it developed into such an appropriate and mature feature and was depicted in a drawing representing what we may take to be a typical scene. The two tiers of jutting *hua-kung* are intersected by transverse *kung*, and the inverted-V intermediate set is also used. The fin-shaped ornaments on the ridge ends and the bud-shaped ornaments on the hips are motifs that have since taken other forms. The only inaccuracy is the excessive slenderness of the columns, which are probably so presented in order not to obstruct the Buddhas and Bodhisattvas depicted within the building.

Other important sources of information are the paintings of the T'ang dynasty recovered by Sir Aurel Stein and Professor Paul Pelliot from the Caves of the Thousand Buddhas (fifth to tenth centuries) at Tun-huang, Kansu Province, now in the British Museum and the Louvre. In these paintings on silk and in the cave mural paintings are scenes representing the Paradise of the West, or the Happy Land of Amitabha. Many are set against highly architectural backgrounds of halls, towers, pavilions, pagodas, and the like. Here the *tou-kung* are seen not only with the outstretching *hua-kung*, but with the beveled ends of the slanting *ang*, a mode of construction employing the principle of the lever to make possible the far overhang of the eave, a device found in most of the monumental buildings of later periods. A great many other details can be gathered from these paintings (fig. 23).

In some cave temples of the late T'ang dynasty in Szechuan Province, scenes of the same theme are shown in relief. The architecture depicted there is far simpler than that in the paintings, undoubtedly due to the limitations imposed by the medium. We can therefore infer, by comparing the sculptured and painted representations of this one theme, that the architecture depicted in the Han tombs and in the caves of the Wei, Ch'i, and Sui dynasties must have been a simplified version of a much more fully developed timber original.

A temple hall of the T'ang
dynasty, engraved relief from
the Ta-yen T'a (Wild Goose
Pagoda), Sian, Shensi, 701–704

A TEMPLE HALL OF THE T'ANG DYNASTY
AFTER A RUBBING OF THE ENGRAVING ON THE TYMPANIUM OVER THE WEST
GATEWAY OF TA-YEN T'A, TZ'U-EN SSŬ, SI-AN, SHENSI

唐代佛殿圖　摹自陝西長安大雁塔西門門楣石画像

Monumental Timber–Frame Buildings

23
T'ang architectural details from scrolls discovered in the Caves of the Thousand Buddhas, Tun-huang, Kansu

Fo-kuang Ssu

The oldest wooden structure known today is the Main Hall of Fo-kuang Ssu, in the Wu-t'ai Mountains, Shansi Province (fig. 24).★ Built in 857, twelve years after the last nationwide persecution of Buddhism, it replaced a seven-bayed, three-storied, ninety-five-feet-high hall, which had housed a colossal statue of Mi-le (Maitreya), also destroyed. The existing structure is a single-storied hall of seven bays. It is extremely impressive with its rigorous and robust proportions. The enormous *tou-kung* of four tiers of cantilevers—two tiers of *hua-kung* and two tiers of *ang*—measuring about half the height of the columns, with every piece of timber in the ensemble doing its share as a structural member, give the building an overwhelming dignity that is not found in later structures.

The interior manifests grace and elegance. Spanning the hypostyle columns are "crescent-moon beams," supported at either end by four tiers of *hua-kung* that transmit their load to the columns. In contrast to the severity of the exterior, every surface of the beams is curved. The sides are pulvinated, and the top and bottom are gently arched, giving an illusion of strength that would otherwise be lacking in a simple straight horizontal member.

The building's most significant feature, from the point of view of dating structural evolution, is the formation of the "truss" immediately under, and therefore supporting, the ridge. On the top tier of beams are placed a pair of *ch'a-shou* ("abutting arms") butting against each other to carry the ridge pole, while the "king post" is missing altogether. This is a rare survival of early construction practice. Similar construction is indicated in the Stone shrine at the Tomb of Chu Wei (first century A.D.), Chin-hsiang, Shantung Province (fig. 13), and also in one of the Tun-huang paintings. In actual specimens, it is employed in the colonnade around the courtyard of Horyuji (seventh century), Nara, Japan. The Fo-kuang Ssu example is the only one of its kind preserved in China and is never seen in later structures.

What makes the Main Hall even more of a treasure is the presence within of sculpture, painting, and calligraphy, all of the same date. On the large platform is a pantheon of nearly three dozen Buddhas and Bodhisattvas of colossal and heroic size. Of even more interest are the two humble, life-sized portrait statues, one of a woman, Ning Kung-yu, donor of the Hall, and the other of a monk, Yuan-ch'eng, the abbot who rebuilt the temple after the destruction of 845. On the undersides of the beams are inscriptions written with brush and ink, giving the names of the civil and military officials of the district at the time of the completion of the Hall, and also that of the donor. On one frieze a fresco of moderate dimensions, unmistakably T'ang in style, is preserved. In comparison the Sung painting in the next bay, dated 1122, itself a great treasure, is eclipsed. Thus in a single building are found examples of all four of the

---

★A smaller and simpler temple, Nan-chan Ssu, built in 782, was later discovered in the same region. See article in *Wen Wu* 1 (1954) 1:89.—Ed.

plastic arts of the T'ang dynasty. Any one of them would be proclaimed a national treasure; and the assemblage of all four is an unimaginable extravagance.

The next one hundred and twenty years is a blank period from which not a single existing wooden structure is known. Then there are two wooden structures in the Tun-huang caves, dated 976 and 980. Although they hardly deserve the name of real buildings, for they are merely porches screening the entrances of the caves, nevertheless they are rare examples of the architecture of the early Sung dynasty.

24
Main Hall, Fo-kuang Ssu, Wu-t'ai Shan, Shansi, 857
a
General view. The Main Hall is at upper right; the long roof at left is the later Wen-shu Tien.

b
Facade
c
Exterior *tou-kung*

24
Main Hall, Fo-kuang Ssu
d
Front interior gallery. Liang at
tripod in foreground.
e
Inside of hypostyle

f
Interior of *tou-kung* and T'ang
mural
g
Roof frame

h
Statue of lady donor
i
Statue of abbot

48
Monumental Timber-Frame
Buildings

24
Main Hall, Fo-kuang Ssu
j
Elevation and longitudinal
section
k
Plan and cross section

LONGITUDINAL SECTION　縱斷面　　西立面　WEST ELEVATION

山西五台山　佛光寺大殿　唐大中十一年建　857 A.D.

MAIN HALL of FO-KUANG SSU · WU-T'AI SHAN · SHANSI

山西五台山 佛光寺大雄寶殿 唐大中十一年建 爲國內現存最古木構

MAIN HALL OF FO-KUANG SSŬ
WU-T'AI SHAN, SHANSI
T'ANG DYNASTY, 857 A.D.
OLDEST WOODEN STRUC-
TURE EXISTING IN
CHINA.

10 '0尺 0   20M.
平面縮尺   SCALE FOR PLAN

人字形义手承脊榑,國內唯一實例
USE OF 人 "RAFTERS" SUPPORT-
ING RIDGE PURLIN
WITHOUT "KING
POST" IS
UNIQUE
EXAMPLE.

平面圖   PLAN

四椽栿(草栿) "4-RAFTER-BEAM" (ROUGH)

草乳栿

四椽栿(月梁)
CRESCENT-MOON BEAM.
梁下唐人題字 T'ANG CAL-
LIGRAPHY, UNDER SIDE OF BEAM.

乳栿

雙抄雙下昂斗栱

唐代塑像
T'ANG SCUPTURE

唐宋壁画
T'ANG & SUNG
FRESCO ON
FRIEZE

昂首承橝,昂尾壓在草乳栿下.
The eave is held up by the
cantilevers 'ang' whose 'tails'
are held down by the beam.

斷面高縮尺
SCALE FOR SECTION

橫斷面   CROSS SECTION

梁思成等測繪

METERS

MEASURED BY LIANG S·C·

Two Buildings of Tu-le Ssu

25
Kuan-yin Ke, Tu-le Ssu, Chi
Hsien, Hopei, 984
a
General view, facade (eave
props added later)

Chronologically the next wooden structures are the magnificent Kuan-yin Ke, or Hall of Avalokitesvara, and the Main Gate, both of Tu-le Ssu, Chi Hsien, Hopei Province. They were built in 984, when that part of the country was under the occupation of the Liao Tartars. The Hall (fig. 25) is a two-storied structure with a mezzanine story. It houses a colossal clay statue of an eleven-headed Kuan-yin, about fifty-two feet in height, the largest of its kind in China. The two upper floors are built around the statue with a "well" in the middle, forming galleries around the figure's hips and chest. In terms of construction, then, the Hall is built of three tiers of "superposed orders," each complete with column and *tou-kung*. The proportions and details of the *tou-kung* show very little departure from that of the T'ang Main Hall in Fo-kuang Ssu. But here, in addition to the double-*kung*–double-*ang* combination that is used on the upper story, there are, supporting the balcony and the lower eave, *tou-kung* without the *ang*, that is, with horizontal cantilevers only, similar to those depicted in the Ta-yen T'a engraving (fig. 22). The interior is a grand exhibition of *tou-kung* of various combinations and in various positions, each arranged so as to do its share in supporting the entire structure. A straight girder, which has taken the place of the "crescent-moon beam," supports the coffered ceiling of very small checkered squares. For carrying the load of the ridge pole, a "king post"—here a *chu-ju-chu* or "dwarf post"—is introduced in addition to the pair of *ch'a-shou*, forming a simple truss. In due course the king post became the sole transmitter of the weight of the ridge pole to the beam, with the total elimination of the *ch'a-shou* truss arms. Thus the presence or absence of the *ch'a-shou* and their size, in proportion to that of the *chu-ju-chu* king post, often serve as convenient criteria for dating a building.

Another characteristic of this period, with rare exceptions, is that the interior or hypostyle columns are usually of the same height as the outer peristyle. The higher parts of the roof frame are supported by the stacking up of *tou-kung*. The columns are seldom lengthened, as is the practice of later ages, to reach for a closer contact with the upper members.

b
Model, showing structural
details
c
Exterior *tou-kung*
d
Interior well

25
Kuan-yin Ke, Tu-le Ssu
e
Kuan-yin statue from below
f
Interior, upper story

KUAN-YIN KÊ
THE HALL OF THE
ELEVEN-HEADED KUAN-YIN
TU-LÊ SSU, CHI HSIEN, HOPEI

LIAO DYNASTY, 984 A.D.

河北 薊縣
獨樂寺 觀音閣
遼統和二年建

义予巨大,与侏儒柱生用.
Small 'King-post' used
in 'truss'.

平梁

Tails of 'Ang' held
down by beam.

四椽栿   (草栿)

乳栿 (草栿)

STATUE IS
LAGEST CLAY
FIGURE IN
CHINA.

昂尾壓在
草栿下.

乳栿
(明栿.魚梁)

斗子蜀柱勾欄

像爲國内最大塑像

平坐柱

全閣結構由三
層斗拱梁柱之
墻架相叠而成.

The entire structure
consists of 3 tiers of
'superposed orders'.

下層平面圖 GROUND FLOOR PLAN

平面縮尺 SCALE FOR PLAN

5M.
0
5
10
15
尺

斷面縮尺

1M
0
5

斷面縮尺 SCALE FOR SECTION

10尺R

斷面圖   CROSS SECTION

g
Plan and cross section

The Shan-men or Main Gate (fig. 26) of Tu-le Ssu is a small structure with very simple *tou-kung* under the eaves. The plan is typical of the Chinese gate building. Along the exterior longitudinal axis is a row of columns on which the doors are fixed. The interior treatment is the so-called open-frame construction, that is, there is no ceiling and all the structural members that support the roof are exposed. Here is exhibited an ingenious example of the carpenter's art, entirely structural in function but extremely decorative in appearance. This dual quality is the greatest virtue of the Chinese structural system.

Starting with these two buildings, we know of more than three dozen timber structures built during the next three hundred years, which include the Liao, Sung, and Chin dynasties. Though their number is small and their chronological distribution uneven, we can still arrange them into a continuity with no unbridgable gaps. About a dozen examples belong to what we call the Period of Vigor, and they are all found in the Liao domain in North China.

The Liao timber structure that follows chronologically the Kuan-yin Ke and Main Gate of Tu-le Ssu is the Main Hall of Feng-kuo Ssu (fig. 27), I Hsien, Liaoning Province, built in 1020. In this large building outside the Great Wall, the intermediate bracket set is identical with the column set, which is a double-*kung*–double-*ang* combination, like that of the column sets of the Kuan-yin Ke. The corner set is further elaborated by placing an auxiliary *lu-tou* on the corner column at each side of the angle, i.e., combining two intermediate sets with the corner set. This treatment, known as the *fu-chiao lu-tou*, or corner set with adjoining *lu-tou*, is quite common later but extremely rare in this early period (fig. 30i).

The San-ta-shih Tien, or Hall of the Three Bodhisattvas (1025), Kuang-chi Ssu, Pao-ti, Hopei Province, is very severe in external appearance but extremely elegant in interior treatment (fig. 28). The bracketing is quite simple: only horizontal *hua-kung* are used. The interior is of the open-frame type, with no ceiling to conceal the structural features. This treatment gives the architect a grand opportunity to display his ingenuity in handling major carpentry as an artistic creation.

26

Main Gate (Shan Men), Tu-le Ssu

a

General view from the inner courtyard

b

Detail of ridge-end ornament.
To the fin shape common in the
T'ang, Sung, and Liao dynasties
is added a dragon's head biting
the ridge with wide-open jaws.
The upper tip of the fin turns
inward and down, a
characteristic that was modified
in fifty years and later
drastically changed.

c

Plan and cross section

河北 薊縣
獨樂寺 山門
遼統和二年建

父子雄大
侏儒柱矮小

托腳雄大,直接托樑

各梁均由斗栱承托

内柱与檐柱同高

SHAN-MEN OR MAIN ENTRANCE GATEWAY
TU-LÊ SSU, CHI HSIEN, HOPEI.
LIAO DYNASTY, 984 A.D.

large "top-chords"
Small "King-post."

large tó-chiao directly
supporting purlin.

All beams
rest on brackets.

Interior columns same
height as exterior
columns.

1 公尺
SCALE FOR SECTION
0
斷面縮尺
4 M.

斷面畫 CROSS SECTION

平面畫   PLAN

公尺 5   0   10M
平面縮尺   SCALE FOR PLAN

27
Main Hall, Feng-kuo Ssu, I
Hsien, Liaoning, 1020
a
General view
b
Exterior *tou-kung*. The plate
above the lintel signals the
beginning of a practice that
became very common after the
Chin dynasty, ca. 1150 (see fig.
38)

28
San-ta-shih Tien, Main Hall,
Kuang-chi Ssu, Pao-ti, Hopei,
1025. (Destroyed)
a
Exterior view
b
Plan and cross section. In this
small Liao building the exterior
tou-kung have no slanting *ang*.
The ties and beams in the
interior are assembled with
tou-kung at their points of
junction.

河北 寶坻縣
廣濟寺三大士殿
遼太平五年建

SAN-TA-SHIH TIEN
OR THE HALL OF THE THREE BODDHISATVAS
KUANG-CHI SSU
PAO-TI, HOPEI

LIAO DYNASTY, 1025 A.D.

义手托脚皆渐见缩小·
"Top-chords" & to-chiao
become smaller.
To-chiao used only here
not found here
僅下平槫用托脚·
中上平槫未用
平梁下用襻間
駝峯下施斗 均罕見

內柱增高以加強與梁之關係
Interior column carried
higher up to make closer
contact with beam.

Use of auxillary tie under beam &
block under "camel-hump"
are rare.

當心間前內柱
向後移一架以
增大前外槽面積
以便獻拜·
Columns placed
backward to
make room for
worship.

平面圖 PLAN

'ÔR 5   0   10M.

平面縮尺 SCALE FOR PLAN

'ÔR 1 0   5 METRES
斷面縮尺 SCALE FOR SECTION

斷面圖 CROSS SECTION

Two Groups at Ta-t'ung

In the city of Ta-t'ung, Shansi Province, are two groups of buildings of great importance—the Hua-yen Ssu, inside the West Gate, and the Shan-hua Ssu, inside the South Gate. Both temples are recorded as having been founded in the T'ang dynasty, but the existing structures date only from the middle of the Liao dynasty.

The Hua-yen Ssu was originally a large temple spreading over a broad acreage. It suffered much damage during the successive frontier wars, and now only three buildings of the Liao and Chin dynasties remain. Among these, the Library (figs. 29a–d) and its Side Hall are two Liao structures, the former dated 1038 and the latter probably constructed at the same time. (The Main Hall of Hua-yen Ssu, which is now the principal building of the so-called Upper Temple, belongs to the next period.)

The bracketing in the Library is similar to that in the Pao-ti structure, but the interior framing is all hidden by the ceiling. Lining the side and back walls are sutra shelves, highly architectural in treatment and exquisitely executed. They are invaluable not only as specimens of cabinetwork of that period, but also as examples of what the *Ying-tsao fa-shih* calls the *pi-tsang*, or wall sutra cabinet. They are excellent models for the study of Liao construction. The Library also houses a group of superb Buddhas and Bodhisattvas.

The Side Hall of the Library is a modest structure with an overhanging gable roof. The bracketing is very simple. Especially noticeable is the use of a *t'i-mu* in the *lu-tou* as an auxiliary half-*kung* under the *hua-kung*, a peculiarity found only in a few buildings of the Liao period and never seen again (fig. 29e).

One other unusual feature of the Hua-yen Ssu group is its orientation. In contrast to the orthodox practice of orienting principal buildings to the south, here the principal buildings face the east. This was an early custom of the Khitans (Liao Tartars), who were originally sun worshippers and considered East the most noble of the four cardinal points.

山西大同華嚴寺薄伽教藏殿

正立面

29
Library, Hua-yen Ssu
b
Elevation of interior wall sutra
cabinet

山西大同華嚴寺薄伽教藏殿壁藏
斷面立面圖

c
Detail of cabinetwork, arched bridge
d
Detail of cabinetwork, showing diagonal *hua-kung*, one of the earliest appearances of this architectural form

front view

purlin

t'i-mu

side view

e
T'i-mu in the Library Side Hall brackets

The Shan-hua Ssu is a group that has retained much of its original arrangement (figs. 30a, b). As the existing buildings show, the original parti consisted of seven principal buildings on one main axis and two transverse axes. The whole group was originally surrounded by a continuous veranda, which is now discernible only by its foundations. Of the seven buildings only one, a flanking tower in the inner courtyard, was destroyed, and the existing ones are all early structures of either the Liao or the Chin dynasties. The connecting galleries and the monks' living quarters have vanished.

The Main Hall and the P'u-hsien Ke belong to the Period of Vigor. The Main Hall (figs. 30c–e) is a seven-bayed structure elevated on a high platform. It is flanked on its left and right by two aligned *to-tien*, or "ear halls"; all three buildings face south. This aligned arrangement of ear-halls is in accordance with ancient tradition and is seldom seen in later buildings. The bracketing of this large structure is quite simple. One significant characteristic is the use of diagonal *kung* in the intermediate sets of the three central bays, which was first seen in the sutra cabinet in the Library of Hua-yen Ssu (fig. 29b) and was to become quite a fad in the Chin dynasty. The adobe wall is reinforced with horizontal courses of wooden "bones," which are effective in preventing vertical cracks. This method was employed in some buildings of the thirteenth and fourteenth centuries, but it was not generally adopted.

The P'u-hsien Ke, or Hall of Samantabhadra (figs. 30f–h) is a two-storied building, very small, but constructed essentially in the same manner as the Kuan-yin Ke of Tu-le Ssu. The diagonal *kung* is again seen here.

These two buildings are of the Liao dynasty. Their exact date is unknown, but stylistically they may be placed in the middle of the eleventh century. The Front Hall and the Main Gate of the Shan-hua Ssu belong to the next period and will be discussed below.

30

Shan-hua Ssu, Ta-t'ung, Shansi, Liao and Chin

a

General view

b
Site plan. This plan is typical of
most Chinese temples, Buddhist
or Taoist. The main hall or halls
are placed on the central axis,
minor halls or subsidiary
buildings on transverse axes.
The buildings are usually
connected by galleries and form
a series of rectangular
courtyards.

· PLOT PLAN · SHAN-HUA SSU · TA-T'UNG · SHANSI ·

30
Shan-hua Ssu
c
Main Hall, ca. 1060, rendering

d
Main Hall, roof frame

e
Main Hall, plan and cross
section

山西大同縣
善化寺大雄寶殿
遼中葉建

MAIN HALL
SHAN-HUA SSU,
TA-T'UNG, SHANSI
LIAO DYNASTY, CIRCA 1060.

内柱之分配使前槽用四椽
檐栿,後外槽用乳栿.
Interior columnization
induces asymmetrical
arrangement of
framing.

前内柱之分配使内槽可立像,外槽便於獻拜.
Interior columnization provides
room for both statues & woshippers.

义手比例著小, "Top-chords" small & insignificant in proportion.

托脚竟止不用 To-chiao entirely
eliminated.

平梁
四椽栿
六椽栿

剳牵
四椽檐栿

乳栿

平面圖
PLAN

内柱亦承六
椽栿中段.
Interior column
supports main
beam at inter-
mediate point.

断面圖   CROSS SECTION

營造尺10   0   20 M.
平面縮尺   SCALE FOR PLAN

營造尺1 0   5   10 METRES.
断面縮尺   SCALE FOR SECTION

30
Shan-hua Ssu
f
P'u-hsien Ke (Hall of
Samantabhadra), ca. 1060
g
P'u-hsien Ke, rendering

山西大同善化寺普賢閣

縱斷面

公 1　0 5 metre
尺

山西大同善化寺普賢閣

h
P'u-hsien Ke, cross section
i
Plan and section of a *fu-chiao
lu-tou* (corner set with adjoining
lu-tou)

The Fo-kung Ssu Wooden Pagoda

The Wooden Pagoda of Fo-kung Ssu, Ying Hsien, Shansi Province (fig. 31), may be considered the grand finale of the Period of Vigor. It was built in 1056 and may have been a fairly common type at that time, for there are quite a few brick versions of it in the provinces of Hopei, Jehol, and Liaoning, then a part of the Liao domain (see map).

The structure is octagonal in plan, with two rings of columns. Its five stories are built entirely of wood. It is similar to the Kuan-yin Ke of Tu-le Ssu in principle of construction: since each upper story is underpinned by a mezzanine story, it actually consists of nine tiers of superposed orders. The ground story is surrounded by a peristyle with a lean-to roof all the way around to give the effect of a double eave. The octagonal pyramidal roof of the top story is surmounted by a wrought-iron *sha*, or finial, the tip of which stands 183 feet from the ground. There are altogether fifty-six different combinations of *tou-kung* in this structure, including all the kinds previously mentioned. The student of Chinese architecture can find no better collection for his studies.

31

Wooden Pagoda, Fo-kung Ssu, Ying Hsien, Shansi, 1056

a

Tou-kung of ground story. The corner set on the obtuse angles necessitated by the octagonal plan is handled on the same principles as the 90-degree-angle corner set. The unrounded end of the lower *hua-kung* is unique.

b

General view

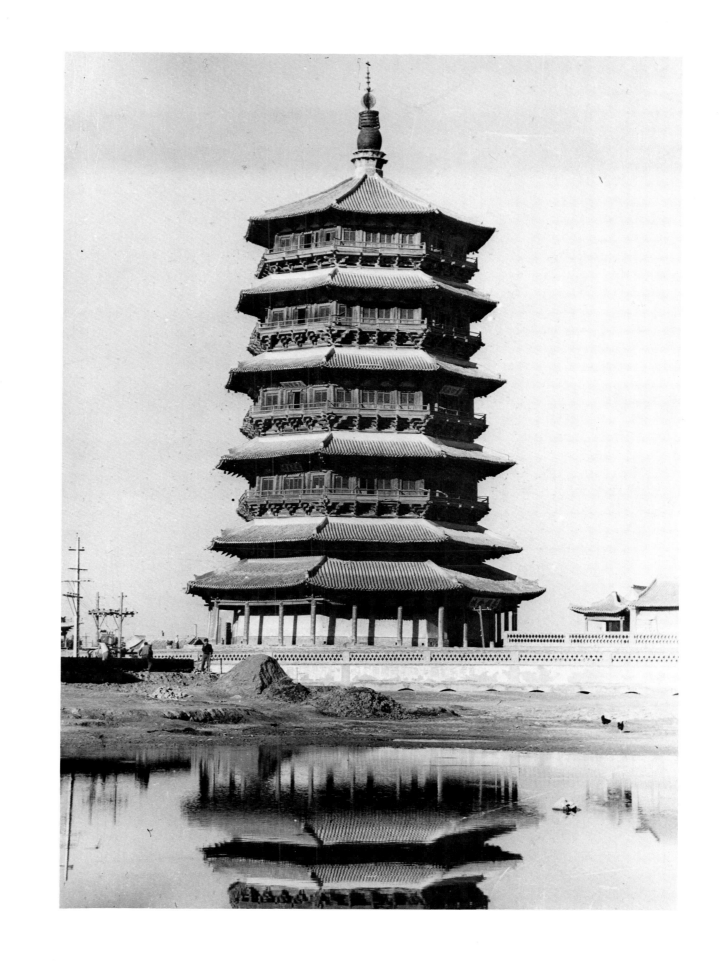

31
Wooden Pagoda, Fo-kung Ssu
c
Rendering

d

Section. The exterior
superposed orders are set back
slightly on each floor so that the
building tapers from base to
top, but except for the top
floor the inside columns are
carried up in a continuous line.
The eaves of the two lower
stories are supported by *tou-
kung* with two tiers of *hua-kung*
and two tiers of *ang*; the three
upper stories and all the
balconies use *hua-kung* only.

山西應縣佛宮寺遼釋迦木塔

中國營造學社測繪　民國廿三年九月實測　廿四年六月製圖

The Period of Elegance (ca. 1000–1400)

Early Sung Characteristics

While the Liao Tartars were carrying on the rigorous traditions of the T'ang dynasty, the Sung architects were already introducing a style characterized by elegance and refinement. This period lasted for approximately four hundred years.

The most noticeable stylistic evolution is the gradual diminution of the *tou-kung*, which were reduced from generally about one third the height of the column to about one fourth by 1400 (fig. 32). The intermediate set becomes relatively larger in size and more complicated in combination and, finally, not only assumes a shape exactly like that of the column set but even further complicates itself by the introduction of the diagonal *kung*. This intermediate set, because it supports no beams and does not rest on a column, becomes a burden to the architrave. In some cases, and also according to the *Ying-tsao fa-shih*, two intermediate sets are used in the central bay. When an *ang* is used in an intermediate set, it further complicates the structural problem by the presence of its tail extending upward at an angle. When used in a column set, the tail is usually held in position by the weight of the beam, but here the tails are cleverly used as intermediate supports for the purlin above. The *ang's* disposition gives the architect a wonderful opportunity to display his ingenuity, resulting in various combinations of great interest. However, the structural function is never forgotten; the sets are always designed to do their share in upholding the whole structure and are seldom idle or merely decorative.

In the interior the columniation is often adjusted to suit a utilitarian purpose, such as providing space to accommodate Buddhist images or worshippers. When columns are omitted in the hypostyle, not only is the plan affected but even the roof framing. (Specific examples will be discussed below.) In addition to this irregularity in columniation, the columns of the hypostyle are increased in height to form a more direct support to the beams above. Yet wherever a horizontal is joined to a vertical member, a simple set of *tou-kung* is always employed as a transition.

In buildings with ceilings, the framework hidden above is generally unfinished or rough. But a monumental building with open framework usually displays a maze of beams, lintels, ties, *tou* and *kung*, and tails of *ang*, interlacing, intersupporting and interdepending. Their disposition is an art in which the architects of this period excelled.

山西五臺山　佛光寺大殿　大中十一年
唐
T'ANG
A.D. 857
MAIN HALL, FO-KUANG SSU,
WU-T'AI SHAN, SHANSI

河北薊縣　獨樂寺觀音閣　統和二年
遼
LIAO
984
KUAN-YIN KÊ, TU-LÊ SSU
CHI HSIEN, HOPEI

山西榆次縣　永壽寺雨花宮　大中祥符元年
宋
SUNG
1008
YÜ-HUA KUNG, YUNG-SHOU SSU
YÜ-TZ'Ŭ, SHANSI

河南登封縣　少林寺初祖庵　宣和七年
宋
SUNG
1125
CH'U-TSU AN, SHAO-LIN SSU
TENG-FENG, HONAN.

山西大同縣　善化寺三聖殿　天會皇統閒
金
CHIN
1130-43
SHAN-SHENG TIEN, SHAN-HUA SSU
TA-T'UNG, SHANSI

山東曲阜縣　孔廟金碑亭　明昌六年
金
CHIN
1195
STELE PAVILION
CONFUCIUS' TEMPLE
CH'Ü-FOU, SHANTUNG

河北正定縣　陽和樓　元初
元
YUAN
CA. 1250
YANG-HO LOU
CHENG-TING, HOPEI

北平　社稷壇享殿　永樂十九年
明
MING
1412
MAIN HALL, SHÊ-CHI T'AN
PEIPING

公尺 1　0　　　　　5 M.
縮尺　SCALE

北平　智化寺如來殿　正統八年
明
MING
1443
JU-LAI TIEN, CHIH-HUA SSU
PEIPING

山東曲阜縣　孔廟奎文閣　弘治十七年
明
MING
1504
LIBRARY, CONFUCIUS' TEMPLE
CHÜ-FOU, SHANTUNG

北平　清故宮文淵閣　乾隆四十年
清
CH'ING
1776
IMPERIAL LIBRARY,
IMPERIAL PALACES, PEIPING.

歷代斗拱演變圖
EVOLUTION
OF
THE
CHINESE
"ORDER"

A Vanguard: Yu-hua Kung

Yu-hua Kung, the small hall of Yung-shou Ssu, near Yu-tz'u, Shansi Province, is a structure in which elegance is most skillfully blended with vigor (fig. 33). Because of its early date (1008) it could be listed among the structures of the preceding period. But here are seen the first signs of the mellowness that will soon characterize the architecture of the Sung and Yuan dynasties. It is a specimen of the transition, embodying the virtues of both periods.

The hall's moderate size and dilapidated condition do not impress the casual onlooker. But its delightful beauty can never escape the eyes of the connoisseur. The *tou-kung* are extremely simple—single *hua-kung* and single *ang*—with the *shua-t'ou*, or head of the beam, shaped like an *ang* and installed in a slanting position to give the effect of two beaks. The set is proportionately large, less than one-third the column height, and the intermediate set is virtually eliminated. In the open-framework interior the exposed members, including the tail of the *ang*, are so neatly joined and fitted that they seem the outcome of an imperative logical sequence.

33
Yu-hua Kung, Yung-shou Ssu,
near Yu-tz'u, Shansi, 1008.
(Destroyed)
a
General view
b
Framing over porch

立面之半 HALF ELEVATION   縱斷面之半 HALF LONGITUDINAL SECTION

山西榆次縣　永壽寺雨華宮　宋大中祥符元年建
YÜ-HUA KUNG · MAIN HALL OF YUNG-SHOU SSU
YÜ-TZ'U · SHANSI · 1008 A·D·

c
Elevation and longitudinal
section

山西 榆次縣

承壽寺 雨花宮

宋大中祥符元年建

YÜ-HUA KUNG
YUNG-SHOU SSU
YÜ-TZ'Ŭ, SHANSI.
SUNG DYNASTY
1008 A.D.

King-post more robust than earlier speciemens

侏儒柱較前期增大

昂尾壓在梁首之下.

Tail of *ang* held in place by beam

四椽栿 Beam of '4-rafter-length' with intermediate support.

要頭斜置作昂嘴形

False *ang*

第一層梁前用乳栿

Front & Rear beams supported where ends meet.

第一層梁後用四椽搭栿

單抄單下昂斗拱

內柱與檐柱同高

Interior & exterior columns of same height.

平面畫 PLAN

尺 5 0 10M

平面縮尺 SCALE FOR PLAN

尺 1 0 5 METRES

斷面縮尺 SCALE FOR SECTION

斷面畫 CROSS SECTION

33
Yu-hua Kung, Yung-shou Ssu
d
Plan and cross section

A Group in Cheng-ting

The Lung-hsing Ssu, Cheng-ting, Hopei Province, is a temple where a number of early Sung buildings is preserved. The Shan-men, or Main Gate, though in a fair state of preservation, was badly repaired in the eighteenth century, when small sets of *tou-kung* in the Ch'ing style were "smuggled" into the spaces between the large original Sung sets. The general aspect is ludicrous.

The Mo-ni Tien is the Main Hall of this temple (figs. 34a, b). It is a double-eaved structure, nearly square in plan. On each of its four fronts is a projecting portico, with its gable-hip roof facing out. This treatment is often depicted in ancient paintings but rarely seen in existing structures. The *tou-kung* are very large and robust. Although there is only one intermediate set in each bay, the diagonal *kung*, which was a favorite of the Liao architects, is used. The very marked "crescendo" of the height of the column toward the corners has a soothing effect.

The Chuan-lun-tsang Tien (Hall of the Revolving Bookcase) is a library built around a revolving sutra cabinet (figs. 34c–g). Here the spacing of the columns in the interior is modified to accommodate the sutra cabinet. This in turn affects the open-framework roof, in which the numerous structural members are ingeniously fitted together, not unlike a well-performed symphony, in which every part comes in at the precise time and place to achieve a perfect harmony.

The revolving sutra cabinet, an octagonal structure that turns on a pivot, is a unique specimen of its kind. In treatment it is a grand elaboration of the architectural elements, taking the form of a double-eaved pavilion. The lower eave follows the shape of the octagon; the upper eave is circular. Both eaves are treated with elaborate *tou-kung*. Because this piece of cabinetwork is executed in close accordance with the specifications in the *Ying-tsao fa-shih*, it is an invaluable example of Sung construction. Unfortunately it was brutally abused by soldiers when the temple was used as a barracks and had been left in a pitiable state when last seen by the author in 1933.

34
Lung-hsing Ssu, Cheng-ting, Hopei
a
Plan of Mo-ni Tien
b
Mo-ni Tien, Main Hall, early Sung, ca. 1030(?)

七間大殿,平面近正方形, 四面出抱廈,出際向前, 為實物中罕見珍例.

7-bay hall, nearly square in plan, with gabled porches on 4 sides is rare example.

宋(仁宗初年?)建

SUNG DYNASTY (CIRCA 1030?)

'8 R 10   5   0   10   20 METRES

河北正定縣龍興寺摩尼殿平面

34
Lung-hsing Ssu
c
Library, Chuan-lun-tsang Tien (The Hall of the Revolving Bookcase), early Sung, ca. 960–1126
d
Library, plan and cross section. Two interior columns are placed out of line to accommodate the revolving cabinet. This irregularity created a structural problem for the floor above, where the central column stands on a girder. The solution was the introduction of a large truss with chords to divert the load of the beam above to the columns at front and rear. Note that the left chord is the extension of the tail of the *ang*.

河北正定縣 龍興寺
轉輪藏殿 宋建

LIBRARY BUILDING, LUNG-HSING SSU, CHENG-TING, HOPEI
NORTH SUNG DYNASTY 960-1127.

平面及斷面畫中皆顯示特殊結構方法以適應安置轉輪藏之需要.

Both plan & section show departure from ordinary columnization & construction to accommodate housing of revolving book-case.

REVOLVING BOOK CASE
前内柱移向两侧讓出轉輪藏位置

Columns placed off centre to make room for revolving book-case.

轉輪藏

平面圖 GROUND FLOOR PLAN

尺 0   5   10M.
平面縮尺 SCALE FOR PLAN

1 0   5M.
斷面縮尺 SCALE FOR SECTION

用大叉手以減輕下層前内額上之荷載
Truss-like frame to reduce load on beam spanning space over revolving book-case.

"TRUSS"

腰檐不施斗栱

Tou-kung not used on "Waist-eave"

Curved tie to make room for revolving book-case.

彎梁是叉在前内額上
End of curved tie carried by beam.

彎梁讓出轉輪藏位置

Porch in front is extension of ground floor eave.

前廊乃將下層檐延長構成

橫斷面 CROSS SECTION

轉輪藏 REVOLVING BOOK CASE.

34
Lung-hsing Ssu
e
Library, the large truss under
the roof. Note the characteristic
decorative treatment of the
structural members.
f
Library, interior corner *tou-kung*
g
Library, the revolving sutra
cabinet

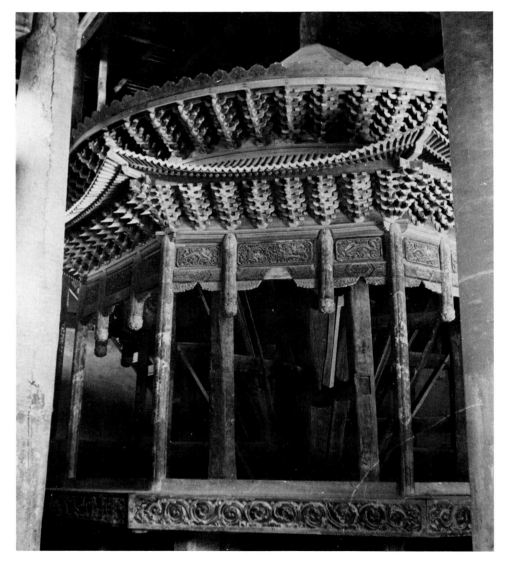

The Chin-tz'u Group

Another important group of the early Sung dynasty is the Sheng Mu Miao, Temple of the Saintly Mother, at Chin-tz'u, near T'aiyuan, Shansi Province (fig. 35). The group consists of a double-eaved Main Hall, reached by a bridge over a rectangular pool, in front of which is a Front Hall and a *p'ai-lou*, and still farther to the front a terrace with four cast-iron guardians. The two halls and the bridge were built in the T'ien-sheng period (1023–1031). Except for the decorative paintings, these structures are well preserved and have been little spoiled by later restorations.

A prominent characteristic of the *tou-kung* of the Lung-hsing Ssu and Chin-tz'u groups is the shape of the beak of the *ang* (fig. 36). In earlier buildings, the beak is a simple bevel, rectangular in cross section, which makes an angle of approximately 25 degrees with the underside of the *ang*. This is known in the *Ying-tsao fa-shih* as the *p'i-chu ang*, or "split bamboo *ang*." But in these two later groups, the beveled portion is scooped and pulvinated, resulting in a cross section with a rounded top, known as the *ch'ing-mien ang*, or "lute-face *ang*." This is the orthodox shape of the beak of an *ang* from the time of the *Ying-tsao fa-shih* till the present day, though later the pulvination is reduced to a mere beveling of the edges. In these two groups the second treatment—the pulvinated straight bevel—characterizes all the *ang*. It is found only in Sung structures of the early eleventh, and possibly the end of the tenth, centuries, for by the time of the publication of the *Ying-tsao fa-shih* (1103), the third treatment was already standardized. The Mo-ni Tien and the Chuan-lun-tsang Tien of Lung-hsing Ssu, and the Wen-shu Tien of Fo-kuang Ssu (see below), are the other surviving buildings that show this second characteristic and are, therefore, of approximately the same date.

Another peculiarity of this short period is the shaping of the *shua-t'ou* in exactly the same manner as the beak of the *ang* (fig. 37). In earlier examples it is usually shaped with either a straight vertical cut or a simple *p'ei-chu* bevel, while later it assumes the form of a "dragon head" or "grasshopper head" (*ma-cha t'ou*). Shaping it exactly like the beak of an *ang* and installing it at a similar angle to create the impression of an extra *ang* are, however, treatments found only in structures built at the turn of the eleventh century.

At this point we may also bring up the *p'u-p'ai fang*, the plate immediately above the lintel (fig. 38). The plate and the lintel are combined to form a T-shaped cross section. Its earliest appearance is in the Yu-hua Kung of Yu-tz'u, Shansi Province (1008), and it is also found in the Cheng-ting and Chin-tz'u groups, but it is comparatively rare in such early structures. Even in the *Ying-tsao fa-shih*, its use is limited to the *p'ing-tso*, or mezzanine story. But by about 1150 the *p'u-p'ai fang* had become an integral part of every building; an architrave without a plate was now an exception.

Another feature of the *tou-kung* that made its debut in the Chin-tz'u structures is the false *ang*. Here the *hua-kung*, a horizontal member, is shaped on the outer end into a beak like that of an *ang*. Thus the decorative effect of the beak is obtained without using the slanting member itself. The *hua-kung* becomes merely an "applied ornament," a sign of degeneration. This treatment eventually became standard in the Ming and Ch'ing dynasties, and its appearance at this very early date is a disheartening portent of the departure from structural integrity that was to come.

35
Sheng Mu Miao (Temple of the
Saintly Mother), Chin-tz'u,
near T'aiyuan, Shansi, early
Sung, ca. 1030
a
Main Hall, general view
b
Main Hall, detail of facade,
showing *tou-kung* and *ang*

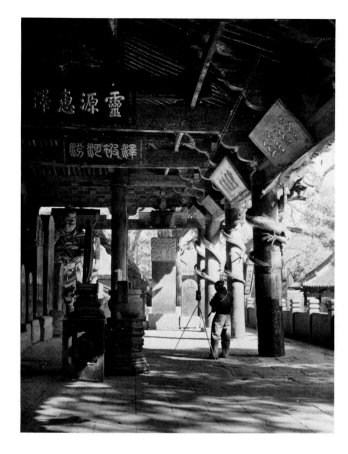

c
Main Hall, interior of porch
d
Front Hall

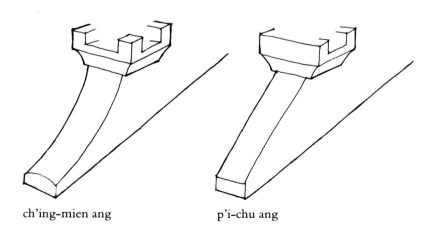

ch'ing-mien ang   p'i-chu ang

36
Changes in shape of beak of the
ang

37
Evolution of the *shua t'ou* (head of the beam)

歷代耍頭(梁頭)演變圖 EVOLUTION OF THE SHUA-T'OU (HEAD OF THE BEAM)

公分 10 0   50   100 cm.

唐	唐	遼	宋
857	857	984	1008
佛光寺正殿	佛光寺正殿	獨樂寺觀音閣	永壽寺 雨華宮
MAIN HALL, FO-KUANG SSU		TU-LÊ SSU	YUNG-SHOU SSU

宋	遼	宋	宋
CA. 1030	1038	1100	1125
佛光寺 文殊殿	薄伽敎藏	營造法式	初祖庵
WEN-SHU TIEN, FO-KUANG SSU	LIBRARY HUA-YEN SSU	YING-TSAO FA-SHIH	CH'U-TSU AN

金	金	金	金
CA. 1130	1118-43	1118-43	1118-43
華嚴寺大殿	善化寺三聖殿	善化寺三聖殿	善化寺山門
MAIN HALL, HUA-YEN SSU	FRONT HALL SHAN-HUA SSU	FRONT HALL SHAN-HUA SSU	MAIN GATE SHAN-HUA SSU

元	明	清	清
CA. 1260-80	1504	1733	1776
陽和樓	奎文閣	工程做法	文淵閣
YANG-HO LOU	LIBRARY CONFUCIUS' TEMPLE	KUNG-CH'ENG TSO-FA CHÊ-LI	WEN-YUAN KÊ

歷代闌額普拍枋演變圖

EVOLUTION OF THE
LAN-ÊH AND P'U-P'AI-FANG
(ARCHITRAVE AND PLATE)

A Unique Construction: Wen-shu Tien

The Wen-shu Tien, or Hall of Manjusri, side hall to the T'ang structure in Fo-kuang Ssu, is a seven-bayed structure, with overhanging gables, of unimposing facade (fig. 39). Its *tou-kung* are similar in treatment to those of Lung-hsing Ssu and Chin-tz'u. It is, however, interesting as a unique example of interior framing. Because of its peculiar columniation, only two hypostyle columns are used in the central bay at the rear, so that the span between them is lengthened to three bays, about forty-six feet from center to center of the columns. No timber of average size could span this length, so a compound framework resembling a modern "queen-post" truss was introduced. However, the construction, which is really no truss in the structural sense, did not live up to the task expected of it by its designer, and an auxiliary support had to be installed in later years.

39
Wen-shu Tien (Hall of
Manjusri), Fo-kuang Ssu
a
General view
b
Interior, showing "queen-post"
truss

內額

义手　綽幕　侏儒柱

由額

Framework resembling a Queen-post Truss to reinforce long lintel. Has highly decorative effect. Unique example.

Auxiliary post added later when 'truss' proved inadequate.

内額与由額之間以綽幕义手，侏儒柱搆作形似近代Queen-post truss之搆架，以輔內額承重，靈巧美觀，為僅見孤例。但仍不勝荷載，後世又加立小柱。

縱斷面畵　LONGDITUDINAL SECTION

山西五台山
佛光寺文殊殿

HALL OF MANJUSRI, FO-KUANG SSŬ.
WU-T'AI SHAN, SHANSI

平面畵　PLAN

M. 5　0　10公尺
平面縮尺 SCALE FOR PLAN

1　0　5公尺 M.
斷面縮尺　SCALE FOR SECTION

c
Plan and longitudinal section

Examples Contemporary with the *Ying-tsao fa-shih*

Of the existing Sung buildings, the one closest to the *Ying-tsao fa-shih* in date is a small hall, the Ch'u-tsu An of Shao-lin Ssu, in the Sung Mountains, Honan Province (fig. 40). It is a square structure of three bays. The stone columns are octagonal; one bears the date 1125, only twenty-two years after the publication of the book. The general structural features abide quite closely to the rules, and the *tou-kung* are executed in almost complete obedience to them. A minor feature revealing a Sung characteristic is the treatment of the sides of the ramps: the triangular walls are treated with a series of sunken panels, one inside another, exactly as specified in the *Ying-tsao fa-shih*.

Farther to the north, in the domain then under the Chin Tartars, are also several buildings of approximately the same date. The Main Hall of Ching-t'u Ssu, (fig. 41), Ying Hsien, Shansi Province, built in 1124, is a year closer in date to the *Ying-tsao fa-shih* than is the Ch'u-tsu An. In spite of the political and geographical distance, the general proportion of this building adheres quite closely to the Sung rules. Its ceiling, treated with the *t'ien-kung lou-ke*, or "heavenly palaces" motif, as given in the *Ying-tsao fa-shih*, is a magnificent piece of cabinetworker's art.

The Front Hall and the Main Gate of Shan-hua Ssu, Ta-t'ung, Shansi Province (fig. 42), in the domain of the Chin Tartars, were built between 1128 and 1143. In the Front Hall the intermediate sets of *tou-kung* with diagonal *kung*, which had previously appeared in the Mo-ni Tien of Lung-hsing Ssu, the Wooden Pagoda of Ying Hsien, and elsewhere, have developed into formidable jumbles of intersecting *kung* and *tou*, imposing themselves as a terrific load on the architrave. The *p'u-p'ai fang*, the plate resting on the lintel, has become thicker than the few examples of earlier dates. In the open-framework interior the *tou-kung* are very effectively employed.

The Shan-men, or Main Gate, of Shan-hua Ssu is perhaps the most pretentious of its kind (fig. 43). The five-bay structure is certainly larger than many a main hall of smaller temples. Its *tou-kung* are simple, and the diagonal *kung* does not appear. The "crescent-moon beam" is used, which is very rare for northern China.

Contemporary with the Chin Tartars was the Southern Sung dynasty. So far only one wooden structure of this period is known in the south: the Main Hall, San-ch'ing Tien, of the Taoist temple Hsuan-miao Kuan, Soochow, Kiangsu Province. Although it was built in 1170, not even three-quarters of a century after the *Ying-tsao fa-shih*, it has lost much of the vigor of that time and appears much more ornate than contemporary and even later structures in the north. The smallness of the *tou-kung* in proportion to the hall as a whole is especially noticeable.

40
Ch'u-tsu An, Shao-lin Ssu,
Sung Shan, Teng-feng, Honan,
1125
a
General view
b
Detail of facade
c
Plan, and intermediate and
column *tou-kung*

河南登封縣少林寺初祖庵   CH'U-TSU AN, SHAO-LIN SSU, TENG-FENG, HONAN

5公尺 0 5M.
平面縮尺 SCALE FOR PLAN

1公尺 0 1M
詳畫縮尺 SCALE FOR DETAIL

全部用八角石柱
All columns of
stone, octagonal.

宋宣和七年建
SUNG DYNASTY
A.D. 1125

北

平面圖
PLAN

補間鋪作
INTERMEDIATE
SET

柱頭鋪作
SET ON
COLUMN

劉敦楨測繪
MEASURED BY LIU T.T.   外檐鋪作   DETAIL, TOU-KUNG SETS

41
Main Hall, Ching-t'u Ssu, Ying
Hsien, Shansi, 1124
a
Facade
b
Ceiling

42
Front Hall, Shan-hua Ssu, Ta-
t'ung, Shansi, 1128–1143
a
General view
b
Detail of facade, showing
diagonal *kung* in intermediate
bracket sets

山西大同善化寺三聖殿

縱斷面

山西大同善化寺
三聖殿

次間橫斷面

公尺 0　　　　　5 metre

42
Front Hall, Shan-hua Ssu
e
Plan and roof framing

43
Shan-men, Main Gate, Shan-
hua Ssu, 1128–1143
a
General view
b
Plan and cross section

山西大同縣 善化寺山門
金天會八年至皇統三年間建

ENTRANCE GATEWAY
SHAN-HUA SSU
TA-T'UNG, SHANSI
CHIN DYNASTY
BETWEEN 1130 & 1143.

凡門屋大多在縱中線上立柱
Gateways generally have row of
columns on longitudinal axis.

平面圖 PLAN

尺 5 0 10M.
平面縮尺 SCALE FOR PLAN

善化寺金代殿堂為与宋李誠營造法式約略同時之實例

The Chin buildings of Shan-hua Ssŭ
are the few speciemens nearly
contemporary to the Ying-tsao-fa-
shih, treatise on architecture by
Li Chieh, architect to Emperor
Hui-tsung, 1101-1126 A.D.

月梁 CRESCENT MOON BEAM

月梁之應用,自宋以
後,北方已極罕見。
The "crescent-moon beam"
is rarely used in North
China since the Sung
Dynasty.

斷面圖 CROSS SECTION

斷面縮尺 尺 0   5M. SCALE FOR SECTION

The Last Phase of the Period of Elegance

Quite a number of specimens in both the north and the south survive from the last century and a half of the Period of Elegance. During this time the *tou-kung* underwent many important changes. One was the widespread use of the false *ang*, which first appeared in the Chin-tz'u group. Another was the increasing size of the *shua-t'ou*, the "grasshopper-head" outer beam-end, on the column set (see fig. 37). As the *tou-kung* shrank through the ages, the *shua-t'ou*, when cut to the ancient proportion of one *ts'ai*, proved too flimsy for its structural function; so, proportionally, it had to become larger than one *ts'ai*. In order to receive it, the *hua-kung* underneath also had to become wider. (By the time of the *Kung-ch'eng tso-fa tse-li* of 1734, the *shua-t'ou* on the column set had swollen in width to 40 *fen*, or four *tou-k'ou*, four times the Sung proportion. The width of the lowest tier of *hua-kung* had become twice its ancient width, from ten *fen* to 20 *fen*, or two *tou-k'ou*.)

The Yang-ho Lou of Cheng-ting, Hopei Province (ca. 1250) is an excellent example of the last phase of the Period of Elegance. It is a seven-bayed structure, a sort of belvedere on a high masonry terrace, which is penetrated by two vaulted tunnels like a city gate, standing as a monumental feature over the main thoroughfare of the city (fig. 44). The *tou-kung* appear to be double *ang*, but in reality both tiers of *ang* on the column set are false, and on the intermediate set one is false and one real. The architrave is pulvinated and shaped at both ends like the crescent-moon beam, but of course it is not arched. This treatment is found in a few other buildings of the Yuan dynasty.

Among other examples are the Te-ning Tien, Main Hall of the Pei-Yueh Miao (1270), Ch'u-yang, Hopei Province (fig. 45), and the Ming-ying-wang Tien of the Temple of the Dragon King at Kuang-sheng Ssu (ca. 1320), Chao-ch'eng, Shansi Province (fig. 46). The latter is decorated with a mural painting representing a theatrical performance of the Yuan dynasty, dated 1324, a rare example of a secular subject used in the decoration of a religious building.

44
Yang-ho Lou, Cheng-ting,
Hopei, ca. 1250. (Destroyed)
a
General view

b
Plan and cross section

YANG-HO LOU, CHENG-TING, HOPEI.

LATE CHIN OR EARLY YUAN

CIRCA 1250?

平面圖   PLAN

河北正定縣 陽和樓 元建
或金末

5公尺
斷面縮尺
SCALE FOR SECTION

20公尺
平面縮尺
SCALE FOR PLAN

0

M.I   10

0

斷面圖   SECTION

45
Te-ning Tien, Main Hall, Pei-
yueh Miao, Ch'u-yang, Hopei,
1270
a
General view
b
Interior view of *tou-kung*
supporting porch roof
c
Plan

46
Ming-ying-wang Tien (Temple
of the Dragon King), Kuang-
sheng Ssu, Chao-ch'eng,
Shansi, ca. 1320

The Upper Temple and the Lower Temple of Kuang-sheng Ssu, Chao-ch'eng, Shansi Province, are two interesting groups of which the buildings are constructed in a most unorthodox manner (fig. 47). In these late Yuan or early Ming structures are found enormous *ang*, so employed that, in some cases, even beams are dispensed with. Such construction is also found in a few other buildings in southern Shansi, for example, the Temple of Confucius of Lin-fen. But it is not seen in other localities or other periods, therefore it may be a purely local characteristic.

The Main Hall of Yen-fu Ssu (1324–1327), Hsuan-p'ing, Chekiang Province (fig. 48), is a rare specimen of a Yuan building in the Lower Yangtze region and south of the river. The open-framework structure is a masterpiece of intricate carpentry. Though characteristically Yuan, it has a suavity and lightness in prominent contrast to the heavier construction of the north.

There are also a few buildings of the Yuan dynasty in the southwestern province of Yunnan. It is interesting to note that the remote regions, though slow to catch up with the general proportions of structures in the eastern cultural centers, were quite apt in copying details of the contemporary period. The Yunnan buildings are twelfth or thirteenth century in general proportion but fourteenth century in treatment of details.

47
Kuang-sheng Ssu, Chao-ch'eng,
Shansi, late Yuan or early Ming
a
Main Gate

d
Upper Temple hall
e
Upper Temple interior,
showing huge *ang*

b
Lower Temple hall, 1319
c
Lower Temple interior,
showing huge *ang*

48
Main Hall, Yen-fu Ssu, Hsuan-
p'ing, Chekiang, 1324–1327
a
General view
b
Interior view of *tou-kung*

With the founding of the capital at Peking at the beginning of the fifteenth century, there appeared, principally in the official architecture of the court, a style of marked departure from the tradition of the Sung and Yuan dynasties. The change is very abrupt, as if some overwhelming force had turned the minds of the builders toward an entirely new sense of proportion. Even during the reign of Emperor Hung-wu (1368–1398), founder of the Ming dynasty, buildings were still constructed in the Yuan style. A few good examples of this last flicker of the Period of Elegance are the City Gates (1372) and the Drum Tower (probably also 1372) of Ta-t'ung, Shansi Province, and the Fei-lai Tien of Fei-lai Ssu (1391), O-mei, Szechuan Province.

The sudden change in the proportion of the *tou-kung* in the structures of the new capital is at once noticeable (see fig. 32). Measuring about one-half or one-third the height of the column in the Sung dynasty, they are in the Ming suddenly shrunken to one-fifth. The number of intermediate sets, never exceeding two in the twelfth century, has now increased to four or six, and later to even seven or eight. Instead of sharing the duty of lifting the overhanging eave, which they can no longer do by means of nimble "jumps," they impose themselves as a load on the architrave. The architrave, which used to be more of a tie than a girder in the previous periods, must now be enlarged to carry this additional load. The *p'u-p'ai fang* no longer forms a 'T' with the architrave, but is flush with it, or even narrower in some cases, for the small *lu-tou* of a shrunken set does not require a plate of excessive width.

In the *tou-kung* itself other great changes have taken place. The *ang*, with its long tail, has no place in a column set with a disproportionately large beam resting directly on it. The false *ang* is therefore always employed where the effect of *ang* is desired. But in the intermediate sets in the interior, the tail of the *ang* is profusely employed, not as a structural member but as a decorative motif. The tails are embellished with an exuberance of carved and applied ornaments, especially the *san-fu yun*, which was originally a simple wing-shaped transverse member occasionally applied on a *hua-kung* with a "stolen heart" in the Sung dynasty, but is now elaborated into "a cloud cluster" and attached to the tail. These tails, however, are no longer the upper parts of the slanting *ang* whose lower (outer) ends are shaped into beaks. The beak is now the extension of the *hua-kung*, resulting in the false *ang*. The tail has become the extension of a horizontal member, such as the *shua-t'ou* or the *ch'en-fang-tou* (the small tie beam above the *hua-kung*). When these horizontal members are extended by means of a long slanting tail, they become something like a hockey stick in appearance. They are no longer the lever arms that hold up the purlin, but a burden to be supported by an auxiliary lintel. The *tou-kung*, except in the column sets, is therefore by now pure ornament.

In the disposition of beams forming the roof support, the *tou-kung* is dispensed with altogether and the beams, now larger, rest directly on columns or struts. The purlins are supported directly on the ends of the beams, without the assistance of *kung* or the bracing of *ch'a-shou* or *t'o-chiao*. The now sturdy king post supports the ridge purlin alone.

Columniation is so regular that the plan becomes a checkerboard. After about 1400 a column is seldom omitted to make room for a utilitarian requirement.

Emperor Yung-lo's Tomb

The earliest surviving example of this style of architecture is the Sacrificial Hall of the Tomb of Emperor Ch'eng-tsu (Yung-lo), built between 1403 and 1424, at the Thirteen Ming Tombs, Ch'ang-p'ing, Hopei Province. All the subsequent emperors and empresses of the Ming dynasty were buried in this neighborhood, but Yung-lo's tomb was the grandest and dominated at the center.

The Sacrificial Hall (fig. 49), which is the principal building in the tomb compound, is a nine-bayed, double-eaved hall, elevated on three tiers of marble terraces. It is almost an exact replica of the Feng-t'ien Tien, Emperor Yung-lo's audience hall in the Imperial Palaces in Peking (see below). The *tou-kung* are extremely small in proportion, with tails of unprecedented length. As many as eight intermediate sets are used, all of them purely ornamental. Both the small size of the *tou-kung* and the large number of intermediate sets are uncommon in structures of this early phase of the period. The general effect of the building, however, is most impressive.

49
Sacrificial Hall, Emperor Yung-lo's Tomb, the Ming Tombs, Ch'ang-p'ing, Hopei, 1403–1424
a
General view

b
Interior detail of ceiling and
structure
c
Plan and cross section

河北昌平縣　明長陵稜恩殿　明永樂間建

SACRIFICIAL HALL
TOMB OF EMPEROR YUNG-LO
THE MING TOMBS
CH'ANG-P'ING, HOPEI.

BUILT DURING THE REIGN
OF YUNG-LO, 1403-24.

殿身　HALL

月台
TERRACE

三層白石陛
3-tier
marble
terrace.

平面畫　PLAN

10 0   40 M.

平面縮尺　SCALE FOR PLAN

殿為國內最大木構之一,面積僅
略遜於北平故宮太和殿.
The Hall is one of the largest wooden structures
in China. Its superficies is surpassed by
the Tai-ho Tien in the Imperial Palaces, Peiping,
by a narrow margin.

义手托脚巳全部廢除
Diagonal supports
entirely eliminated.

昂長為實物中第一
Longest ang
in existance.

斗栱淪為裝飾,比例甚小.
Tou-kung dwindles into
sheer ornament, small
& insignificant
in proportion
to structure.

丹陛三重,台石欄杆
之最古實例.
Oldest existing example
of triple terrace with
marble balustrade.

斷面畫　CROSS SECTION

斷面縮尺 5 0   10 M. SCALE FOR SECTION

MEASURED BY
THE BUREAU OF CONSTRUCTION
MUNICIPAL GOVERNMENT OF PEIPING

北平市政府工務局測繪

Ming Buildings among the Peking Palaces

The Imperial Palaces of the Ming dynasty at Peking were rebuilt on the ruins of the sacked Yuan capital, the Ta-tu that Marco Polo visited. Since its rebuilding five and a half centuries ago, it has remained little changed in general parti till the present day. Although the Huang-chi Tien (called Feng-t'ien Tien at the beginning of the Ming dynasty and replaced by the T'ai-ho Tien in the Ch'ing dynasty), the principal audience hall, was destroyed at the fall of the Ming dynasty, there are still a considerable number of Ming buildings in the Forbidden City. Of these the Hsiang Tien, or Sacrificial Hall, of She-chi T'an—in the Central Park—is the oldest, built in 1421 (fig. 50). Here the *tou-kung* still measures about two-sevenths the column height, and only six intermediate sets are installed in the central bay, four in the side bays. An interesting group in the Palaces is the Imperial Ancestral Temple, or T'ai Miao, rebuilt principally in 1545 (fig. 51).

The Chien-chi Tien (renamed Pao-ho Tien), the last of the "Three Great Halls," is a structure dating from 1615, rebuilt after a fire (fig. 52). It fortunately escaped destruction when the two halls in front of it were burned down at the fall of the dynasty in 1644 and again in a conflagration in 1679. There is little difference between it and buildings of the period of the *Kung-ch'eng tso-fa tse-li* (1734), either in general proportions or in details. It would have been impossible to ascertain its earlier date had it not been for the inscriptions on the structural members above the ceiling; on each the Ming designation "Chien-chi Tien" and the position of the member is written with brush and ink.

The Library in the Temple of Confucius (1504), Ch'ü-fu, Shantung Province (fig. 53), is an interesting example of a two-storied building in the official style of the Ming dynasty. The influence of this rigid style, however, does not seem to have spread far beyond Peking, or rather, beyond the buildings erected by imperial order and according to official regulations. Elsewhere in the empire architects were given more freedom than in the service of the court. Buildings clinging more or less to older traditions are found all over the country. The T'ien-tsun Tien of Wen-ch'ang Kung, Chih-t'ung, (middle Ming), and the group at Chiu-feng Ssu (1443 and later), Peng-hsi, Szechuan Province, are excellent examples.

50
Hsiang Tien, Sacrificial Hall,
She-chi T'an, Forbidden City,
Peking, 1421

51

T'ai Miao, Imperial Ancestral
Temple, Imperial Palace,
Forbidden City, Peking.
Rebuilt 1545.

52
Pao-ho Tien (formerly Chien-
chi Tien), Imperial Palace,
Peking, 1615. Later rebuilt.

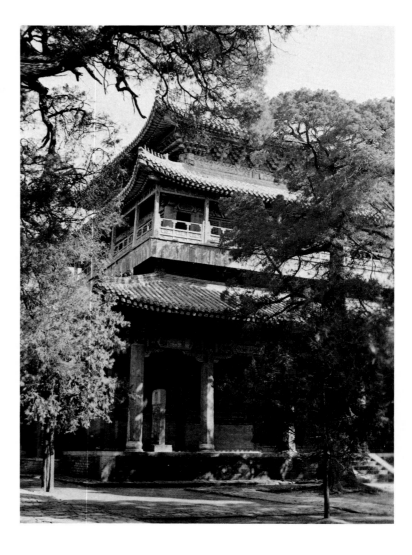

53
Library, Temple of Confucius,
Ch'ü-fu, Shantung, 1504
a
General view
b
Plan and cross section

LIBRARY BUILDING
TEMPLE OF CONFUCIUS
CH'Ü-FOU, SHANTUNG.

MING DYNASTY 1504 A.D.

石柱 STONE COLUMNS

下層平面 GROUND FLOOR PLAN

SCALE FOR PLAN
平面縮尺
5 公尺
0
10 M.

SCALE FOR SECTION
斷面縮尺
5 公尺
0
1 M.

明弘治十七年建

山東曲阜縣孔廟奎文閣

侏儒柱獨承屋脊之重, 义手托脚均廢.
Entire ridge load borne by king-post.
All diagonal bracings & supports eliminated.

梁架結構完全不用斗栱
Roof beam framing completely
done away with tou-kung.

斗栱姜小, 結構義意.
少柱裝飾義意.
Tou-kung small and
insignificant, more
ornamental than
structural
in function.

腰檐斗栱為擎檐
柱上楣子掩蔽
Tou-kung of
"waist eave"
screened
off by
auxiliary
'frieze'.

楣子
擎檐柱

平坐斗栱為裝
大雁翅板掩蔽
Tou-kung support-
ing balcony
screened off
by "clap-board".

雁翅板

平坐內部不施斗栱, 平庭
柱與上層柱通貫為一.
Tou-kung not used in mezzanine
interior. Columns carried thru
two storeys.

石柱
STONE COLUMN

下層則仍全用斗栱, 尚存古制.
Tou-kung still employed on
lower storey, retaining some
structural method of earlier
periods.

普拍枋
闌額

因補間鋪作桨
數加多, 闌額加
大以承其重, 普
拍枋反縮小, 加
厚.

Increase in
number of
intermediate
sets of tou-
kung causes
increase in
size of lintel,
while plate be-
comes thicker
& narrower.

斷面圖 SECTION

Ch'ing Buildings in Peking

The architecture of the Ch'ing dynasty (1644–1912) is a mere continuation of the Ming tradition. With the publication of the *Kung-ch'eng tso-fa tse-li* in 1734, innovation was stifled. In the structures built for the emperors throughout the 268 years of the regime there is a uniformity that no modern totalitarian state could achieve. Most of the buildings in the Imperial Palaces in the Forbidden City and the Imperial Tombs and numerous temples in and around Peking are products of this school (figs. 54–56).

The most outstanding examples are, of course, the Imperial Palaces (fig. 57). As individual buildings, especially from a structural point of view, they are unremarkable. But as a composition of the grand plan, there is nothing comparable to it in the world: it is a grand plan on the grandest scale. The mere idea of laying out an axis nearly two miles in length from south to north, with an endless series of avenues, courts, bridges, gates, colonnades, terraces, pavilions, halls, palaces, balanced with perfect symmetry on both sides, and all built in exactly the same fashion, in strict accordance with the *Kung-ch'eng tso-fa tse-li*, is a most appropriate expression of the Son of Heaven and of a powerful empire. Here, the uniformity induced by the strict rules turns out to be more of a merit than a defect. Without such rigid restrictions, dignity and grandeur of such magnitude could never have been achieved.

There is, however, a grave drawback in this composition. It seems that the planner totally overlooked, or we may venture to say that he was incapable of coping with, the secondary or transverse axes. Even in the grouping of buildings immediately flanking those on the main axis, the relation between the axes is not always comfortable. Thus we find that almost all the groups in the Forbidden City, especially the "apartments" on both sides of the series on the principal axis, though well balanced within the four walls of each group—each with its north and south axis parallel to the main axis of the Forbidden City—bear no definite relation to it transversally. Although this emphasis on one axis is in fact an outstanding characteristic of all Chinese planning, as is shown in all the temples and residences throughout China, it is almost unbelievable that a planner who paid so much attention to symmetry on one axis should have ignored so completely the other.

55
Corner tower of the Forbidden
City, Peking, Ch'ing dynasty
a
General view
b
Exterior *tou-kung*

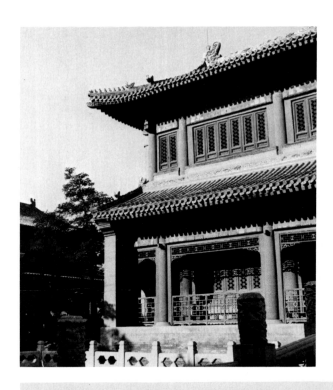

56
Wen-yuan Ke, Imperial
Library, Forbidden City,
Peking, 1776
a
Detail of facade
b
Plan and cross section

57
Imperial Palaces, Forbidden
City, Peking, Ming and Ch'ing
dynasties. Site plan.

1 太和殿
2 中和殿
3 保和殿
4 太和門
5 體仁閣
6 弘義閣
7 昭德門
8 貞度門
9 左翼門
10 右翼門
11 中左門
12 中右門
13 後左門
14 後右門
15 角樓
16 乾清門
17 景運門
18 隆宗門
19 直班房
20 軍機處

北平市清故宮三殿總平面圖

明末及清建

IMPERIAL
PALACES
PEIPING
THE "THREE
GREAT HALLS"
AND
IMMEDIATE
SURROUNDING
BUILDINGS
LATE MING
&
CHING
DYNASTIES

北

The T'ai-ho Tien (Hall of Supreme Harmony), the principal audience hall of the palaces and the focal point of the entire Forbidden City, is the grandest individual building (fig. 58). With its six rows of twelve columns each, forming a hypostyle hall eleven bays in length and five in depth, double-eaved and hip-roofed, it is the largest single premodern building in China. The seventy-two columns, arranged in monotonous regularity that shows any quality except ingenuity, are still a most impressive sight. The hall stands on a low marble platform, which in turn is elevated by three tiers of balustraded terraces, profusely decorated with exquisite carvings. The structure dates back no farther than 1697, built to replace the one destroyed by a fire in 1679.

The *tou-kung* of this gigantic hall are extremely small in proportion—less than one-sixth of the column height. As many as eight intermediate sets are used in one bay. From a distance the presence of *tou-kung* is hardly noticeable. The walls, columns, doors, and windows are painted vermilion, the *tou-kung* and architraves are blue and green accented with gold. The entire structure is crowned by a roof of glazed yellow tiles, glistening like gold in the bright sunshine against the blue northern sky. Surmounting the white marble terraces that seem to vibrate with their exuberant carvings, the great hall is a rare feast for the eye, an unforgettable apparition of grandeur, dignity, and beauty.

As an aside, it may be mentioned that the T'ai-ho Tien is equipped with a most unusual "fire proofing system." In the dark attic under the roof, above the ceiling of the central bay, is a tablet bearing the names and the magic words of both Buddhist and Taoist gods who have control over fire, wind, and the thunderbolt. In front of this tablet stand an incense burner, a pair of candles, and a pair of *ling-chih*, a fungus symbolizing Taoist immortality. So far, the precaution seems to have worked.

58
T'ai-ho Tien, Hall of Supreme
Harmony, Forbidden City,
Peking, 1697
a
General view

b
Marble terraces
c
Ceiling

Another famous building of the Ch'ing dynasty is the Ch'i-nien Tien of the Temple of Heaven (fig. 59). The hall is circular in plan, with three decks of eaves, the uppermost of which forms a conical roof. The glazing of the tiles is blue, the color symbolic of heaven. This beautiful structure is also elevated on three tiers of balustraded marble terraces. The present structure was built in 1890 to replace the one burned down the year before.

A typical Buddhist temple of the Ming and Ch'ing dynasties is the Hu-kuo Ssu in Peking. Founded in the Yuan dynasty, the temple was almost completely rebuilt in the Ch'ing period. The buildings are grouped to allow circulation from one courtyard to another around the sides of the buildings. The drum tower and bell tower standing on the left and right of the forecourt are erected only in temples. One hall in the rear of the compound, a Yuan structure that is now a complete ruin, is an interesting example of the use of timber reinforcements in adobe walls.

A number of mosques were also built in the Ming and Ch'ing dynasties. But except for details in the interior decoration, they show no essential difference from other buildings.

59
Ch'i-nien Tien, Temple of
Heaven, Peking, 1890

The Temple of Confucius, Ch'ü-fu, Shantung

A building almost contemporary with the *Kung-ch'eng tso-fa tse-li* but departing considerably from its rules is the Ta-ch'eng Tien, Main Hall of the Temple of Confucius (1730), Ch'ü-fu, Shantung Province (fig. 60). Although it is impressive for its carved marble columns, in general proportion it has a certain awkwardness not found in other Ch'ing buildings, whether erected by imperial mandate or otherwise.

The Temple of Confucius, which has been in state custody ever since the Han dynasty, is the only group of buildings in China that has an unbroken history for over two thousand years. The present compound is a large group that occupies the entire center of the town of Ch'ü-fu; its present plan was laid out in the Sung dynasty. The numerous buildings within its walls are an interesting assortment of structures of various periods. The oldest is a stela pavilion of the Chin dynasty, 1196, the latest is a building erected in 1933, and examples from the three intervening dynasties—Yuan, Ming, and Ch'ing—are all present.

60

Temple of Confucius, Ch'ü-fu,
Shantung, 1730

a

Ta-ch'eng Tien, Main Hall,
facade

山東曲阜縣
孔廟大成殿
清雍正八年建

TA-CH'ENG TIEN
MAIN HALL OF THE
TEMPLE OF CONFUCIUS
CH'Ü-FOU, SHANTUNG
CH'ING DYNASTY, 1730.

Nearest in date to *Kung-ch'eng-
tso-fa-che-li*, but wide departure from its rules. High pitch
& slight bent give roof-
line appearance of
clumsy rigidity.

單抄三昂斗拱
清代宮式所做
Tou-kung of 1-*kung* &
3-*angs* not in ac-
cordance with
Ch'ing rules.

平面圖 PLAN

ळ尺 5 0   10   20M.
平面縮尺 SCALE FOR PLAN

ळ尺 0   10M.
斷面縮尺 SCALE FOR SECTION

石柱
CARVED
MARBLE
COLUMN

斷面圖 CROSS SECTION

山東曲阜至聖廟平面圖

PLAN,
TEMPLE
OF
CONFUCIUS

CH'Ü-FOU,
SHAN-TUNG

WITH DATES OF
EXISTING BUILD-
INGS FROM 1195
DOWN TILL REC-
ENT YEARS.

60
Temple of Confucius
b
Main Hall, plan and cross
section
c
Plan of entire compound

d
Stela pavilion, plan and cross
section, 1196

STELE PAVILION, TEMPLE OF CONFUCIUS
CHÜ-FOU, SHAN-TUNG, CHIN DYNASTY
1196 A.D.

山東曲阜縣 孔廟碑亭

金明昌六年建？

為聖廟現存最古建築，後世重修，頗
有更改，尤以上層屋頂梁架為
甚。柱額斗栱則大
部仍保持原狀。

Oldest wooden
structure in the Sage's
Temple. Top portion sup-
porting ridge & roof much
altered by later repairs.
Columns, lintels & *tou-kungs*
are mostly original.

此線以上部分清乾隆間改修
Portion above this level
rebuilt in 18th century.

石柱

Stone columns

正心枋正心桁及桁
椀為清官式做法
18th century alteration,
rest of *tou-kung*
original.

平面圖 PLAN

Stone column
石柱

公尺5　　0　　5M.
平面縮尺　SCALE FOR PLAN

公尺1　0　　　3M.
斷面縮尺　SCALE FOR SECTION

斷面圖　CROSS SECTION

Construction Methods in the South

Away from the influence of government regulations, sometimes not even far from Peking, a certain lightness in treatment gives buildings an appearance of liveliness. This manifestation is most pronounced in the provinces south of the Yangtze River. The difference is explained not only by the warmer climate but also by the greater technical agility developed by the southerners. In the milder south there is no necessity for the heavy masonry walls and thick roof construction so imperative for shutting out the severe cold of the north. Walls of plastered laths and roofs with tiles laid directly on rafters without even sheathing are common. Timbers are generally smaller, and roofs often have high up-turned corners that are very playful in spirit. When this tendency is carried to excess, it often results in faulty construction and frivolous ornamentation, at the expense of restraint and purity, two virtues that a good architect can hardly afford to be without.

Residential Architecture

The domestic architecture of the province of Yunnan seems to have struck a happy medium in combining the agility of the south with the restraint of the north. It shows a certain freedom in planning not found in other parts of China. Units of various sizes and functions are joined together, seemingly very casually, with interesting intersections of roofs and romantic fenestrations with "eyebrow eaves" and balconies, often attaining a high degree of picturesqueness in mass composition.

Rural architecture built of local materials, as in the mountain village near Wu-yi, Chekiang Province, is typical of southern China (fig. 61). But in the northern regions of loess plateaus, cave dwellings dug into the loess cliffs are still quite common. In the mountains along the Burma Road in western Yunnan are unusual log cabins, not unlike those of Scandinavia and America in construction. But there is something so essentially Chinese about them, especially in the treatment of the roofing and the porch, that it is hard to deny that an architecture is always permeated with the spirit of its people, as is expressed here even in these out-of-the-way, casual, and modest little cabins (fig. 62).

61

Mountain homes, Wu-i,
Chekiang

62

Log cabin, western Yunnan,
plans and elevations

正面立面 FRONT ELEVATION

側面立面 SIDE ELEVATION

卧室 BED ROOM

卧室 BED ROOM

上

客堂 LIVING ROOM

屋頂 ROOF

廊 PORCH

灶 STOVE

椿 PILES

上層平面 UPPER FLOOR PLAN

下層平面 LOWER FLOOR PLAN

公尺 1 0 5 M.

公尺 1 0 3 METRES

平面縮尺 SCALE FOR PLANS

立面縮尺 SCALE FOR ELEVATIONS

雲南 鎮南縣 馬鞍山

LOG CABIN, MA-AN SHAN, CHEN-NAN HSIEN, YUNNAN

井幹構民居

MEASURED BY LIU T.T.

劉敦楨 測繪

Buddhist Pagodas

As an architectural monument, giving expression and accent to the landscape of China, nothing figures more prominently than the *t'a*, or pagoda. From its first appearance till the present day, the Chinese pagoda has remained essentially "a multi-storied tower surmounted by a pile of metal discs," as we have quoted. It is the happy combination of two principal components: the indigenous "multi-storied tower" and the Indian stupa, the "pile of metal discs." By combinations of the two components, the Chinese pagoda may be classified into four principal types: one-storied, multi-storied, multi-eaved, and stupa. Whatever its size or type, a *t'a* marks the burial site of a Buddhist relic or the tomb of a Buddhist monk.

We know from literary sources such as the citation above, from the replicas in the Caves of Yun-kang (fig. 17), Hsiang-t'ang Shan, and Lung-men, and from existing examples in Japan, that the early pagoda was an indigenous multi-storied tower, square in plan, constructed of timber, and surmounted by a stupa, called the *sha*, or spire. It did not take long for the builders to recognize the advantages of brick and stone for a monument of this kind, and the masonry pagoda soon made its appearance and eventually outlasted its wooden prototypes. With a single exception, the Wooden Pagoda of Ying Hsien (fig. 31), all the pagodas in China today are masonry structures.

The masonry pagoda's evolution (fig. 63) can be divided broadly into three periods: the Period of Simplicity, or the Period of the Square Plan (ca. 500–900); the Period of Elaboration, or the Period of the Octagonal Plan (ca. 1000–1300); and the Period of Variety (ca. 1280–1912). As with our classification of wooden buildings, generous margins must be allowed for the overlapping of, and departure from, stylistic and temporal characteristics.

63
Evolution of types of the
Buddhist pagoda

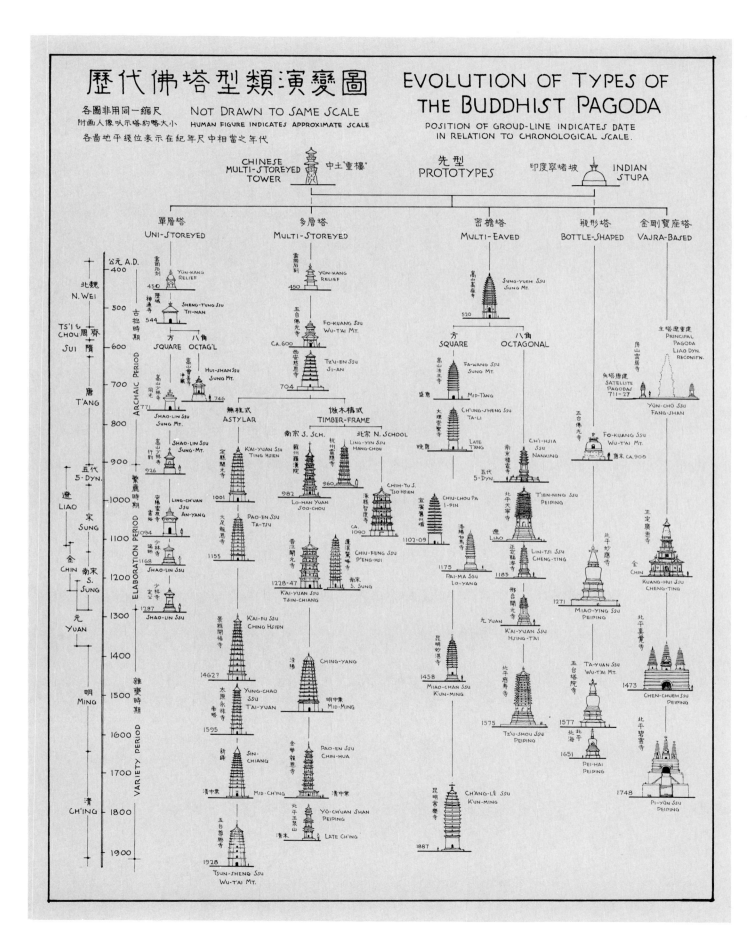

The Period of Simplicity (ca. 500–900)

The first period may be marked from the early sixth century to the end of the ninth century, which includes the Wei, Ch'i, Sui, and T'ang dynasties. The most prominent characteristics, with a few rare exceptions, are the square plan and the one-cell hollow construction; that is, the pagoda is built like a shell, with no internal horizontal or vertical masonry divisions (although there may be wooden floors and stairs). The structure resembles a modern factory smokestack, with the top closed and covered. Three of the four types of pagoda made their appearance in these centuries. The stupa, although an Indian prototype that might be expected in China in this early period, is curiously absent, though there is every reason to believe that it was not unknown. There are many examples of the other three types.

One-storied Pagodas

Pagodas of the one-storied type, with a single exception, are all tomb monuments to deceased monks. They are usually small and are more like shrines than pagodas as the latter term is generally understood. This type is depicted in great numbers in the reliefs of the Yun-kang Caves. It is characterized by a square cella with an arched door-way on one wall, and it is crowned by one or two strings of eaves, or cornices, and is surmounted by a *sha*.

The oldest stone pagoda in China, and the oldest and most important surviving one-storied type, is the Ssu-men T'a (544 A.D.) of Shen-t'ung Ssu, near Tsinan, Shantung Province (fig. 64a). But it is by no means typical because it is neither a tomb monument nor a hollow shell. It is a single-storied, pavilionlike, ashlar structure, square in plan, with a central core surrounded by a gallery, and an arched doorway in each of the four sides. It is the only pagoda of this period with such an interior arrangement, which became the common characteristic of pagodas in the tenth century and thereafter.

Typical examples of the many one-cell tomb pagodas are the Tomb Pagoda of Hui-ch'ung (ca. 627–649) in Ling-yen Ssu, Ch'ang-ch'ing, Shantung Province (fig. 64b), and the Tomb Pagoda of T'ung-kuang (771) in Shao-lin Ssu, in the Sung Mountains, Honan Province (fig. 64c).

A unique specimen of great architectural importance is the Tomb Pagoda of Ching-tsang at Hui-shan Ssu, Teng-feng, also in the Sung Mountains of Honan (figs. 64d, e). Built soon after the death of the monk in 746, it is a small, octagonal, single-storied, pavilionlike brick structure on a high moulding-decorated base, or *shu-mi-tso*. The exterior is treated with engaged columns at the corners, *tou-kung*, false windows, and other elements. The *tou-kung* are similar to those of the Yun-kang and T'ien-lung Shan Caves except for the projection of a *shua-tou*, intersecting the *kung* in the *lu-tou*. An inverted-V intermediate set is placed on the architrave on each face of the octagon. The cella is characteristic of the period, but the octagonal plan and the *shu-mi-tso* appear here for the first time. They are to become the two salient characteristics of pagodas after the latter half of the tenth century. Their introduction in this mid-eighth-century structure presages an important change in the evolution of the pagoda.

64
One-storied Pagodas
b
Tomb Pagoda of Hui-ch'ung,
Ling-yen Ssu, Ch'ang-ch'ing,
Shantung, ca. 627–649
c
Tomb Pagoda of T'ung-kuang,
Shao-lin Ssu, Teng-feng,
Honan, 771

河南登封照會善寺淨藏禪師塔

平面圖

d
Tomb Pagoda of Ching-tsang,
Hui-shan Ssu, Teng-feng,
Honan, 746
e
Tomb Pagoda of Ching-tsang,
plan
f
Tomb Pagoda of Hsing-chun,
Shao-lin Ssu, 926

Multi-storied Pagodas

The multi-storied pagoda, the type most commonly represented in the Yun-kang Caves both in reliefs and in the round, is the superposition of a number of one-storied pagodas. As the structure rises, each story diminishes slightly in both height and breadth. The exterior of the extant brick specimens is often treated with pilasters with a very slight reveal and with simple sets of *tou-kung*, in imitation of the timber construction of the time. The most famous example of this type is the Wild Goose Pagoda, the Ta-yen T'a (figs. 65a, b) of Tzu-en Ssu, Sian, Shensi Province. The original structure, consecrated by the great master Hsuan-tsang in the mid-seventh century, was soon destroyed, and the present structure was built between 701 and 704. Its construction is the typical hollow shell with timber floors and stairways. The exterior is treated with extremely slender pilasters in very delicate relief, in great contrast to the vigorous massive bulk of the structure. A single *tou* is used above each pilaster, and the intermediate set is eliminated. Each side of each story is perforated by an arched doorway. Above the west doorway of the first story is found the valuable engraving depicting a T'ang hall of timber construction (fig. 22).

Two other notable examples of pagodas of this type are the Hsiang-chi Ssu T'a and the Hsuan-tsang T'a, both in the neighborhood of Sian. The Hsiang-chi Ssu T'a (669) is quite similar to the Ta-yen T'a in general parti and in the treatment of exterior walls. But here a single *tou* is used as an intermediate set, and blank windows are represented on the walls (fig. 65c). The Hsuan-tsang T'a in Hsing-chiao Ssu (681) is a small structure of five stories. It may or may not be the tomb monument to the great master. The ground-story treatment is astylar, that is, without columns, while the four upper stories are treated with pilasters. It is similar to the Tomb Pagoda of Ching-tsang in the treatment of *tou-kung*, in which a *shua-t'ou* projects from the *lu-tou*, but here the *shua-t'ou* is vertically cut. This structure, which antedates the Ching-tsang T'a by nearly seventy years, is the earliest specimen showing such a treatment (fig. 65d).

An extremely unusual multi-storied pagoda is the so-called Tsu-shih T'a, or Founder's Tomb Pagoda, of Fo-kuang Ssu, in the Wu-t'ai Mountains, Shansi Province (fig. 65e). Standing a mere few paces to the south of the T'ang Main Hall of 857, it is a two-storied hexagonal structure. The lower story has a cornice of lotus petals and corbelled brick courses, resting on a string of *tou*. (The lotus-petal motif is employed in the treatment of all three tiers of cornices.) The upper story is raised on a *p'ing-tso*, the "mezzanine" or balcony support. This *p'ing-tso* is a *shu-mi-tso*, with "legs" that divide the *shu-yao*, or dado, into small compartments. This treatment of the *shu-mi-tso*, though a minor feature, is one of the most characteristic of the middle and later sixth century, and can be fairly taken as a token of its date. The *p'ing-tso* is an important feature in the structure of a multi-storied building in timber, as we have seen, and its appearance here is significant (fig. 65f).

The upper story is more architecturally treated. The corners are decorated with engaged columns with lotus blossoms at both ends and at the middle, showing an unmistakable Indian influence. The front wall has an arched doorway with a flame-shaped extrados or archivolt, and on each of the two adjacent walls is a window with vertical bars. Above one window an inverted-V intermediate set is still preserved, painted on the plastered wall in dark red (fig. 65g). The drawing has an energetic tension that also characterizes the draperies of the Buddhist sculpture and the calligraphy of the Northern Wei and Ch'i dynasties.

The exact date of this pagoda is not known. But judging from the *shu-mi-tso*, the flame-shaped archivolt, the lotus-blossom column, the inverted-V intermediate set, and other stylistic evidence, it must have been built in the latter part of the sixth century.

65
Multi-storied Pagodas
a
Ta-yen T'a (Wild Goose Pagoda), Tzu-en Ssu, Sian, Shensi, 701–704
b
Ta-yen T'a, plan

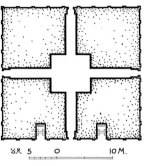

西安慈恩寺大雁塔平面圖

65
Multi-storied Pagodas
c
Hsiang-chi Ssu T'a, Sian,
Shensi, 669

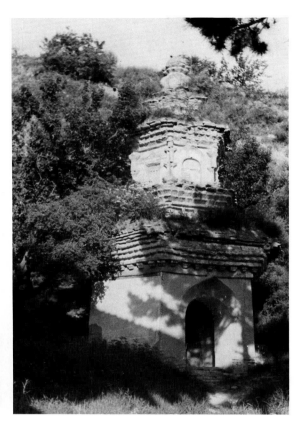

d
Hsuan-tsang T'a, Hsing-chiao
Ssu, Sian, Shensi, 681
e
Tsu-shih T'a, Fo-kuang Ssu,
Wu-tai, Shansi, ca. 600

Chinese labels and annotations (top to bottom, right column of elevation):

賓瓶 'SACRED BOTTLE'
變仰蓮瓣 LOTUS PETALS
覆鉢 'INVERTED ALM BOWL'
雙層仰蓮瓣 LOTUS PETALS
剎 CH'A

屋面 ROOF
三層蓮瓣檐 LOTUS PETAL CORNICE
上層塔身 'BODY' OF UPPER STOREY
上層 UPPER STOREY

三層仰蓮座 LOTUS PETALS
束腰 DADO
下澀 BASE MOULD
平坐 PING-TSO

屋面 ROOF
壺溜檐 CORBELLED CORNICE
蓮瓣檐 LOTUS PETALS
斗 TOU

下層塔身 'BODY' OF GROUND STOREY
下層 GROUND STOREY

TSU-SHIH T'A
FO-KUANG SSU
WU-T'AI SHAN
SHANSI

CH'I OR SUI DYNASTY
CIRCA 600

立面 ELEVATION

山西五臺山 佛光寺 祖師塔

北齊或隋建

4 meters
4 m.

立面縮尺 SCALE FOR ELEVATION
平面縮尺 SCALE FOR PLAN

0 1 5R
0 1 5R

上層平面之半 HALF UPPER STOREY
下層平面之半 HALF GROUND STOREY

PLANS

f
Tsu-shih T'a, plan and elevation
g
Tsu-shih T'a, painted *tou-kung*
over second-story window

Multi-eaved Pagodas

66

Multi-eaved Pagodas

a

Plan of Sung-yueh Ssu T'a

主層 PRINCIPAL STOREY PLAN

河南嵩山嵩嶽寺塔平面

北

1M
0

5尺

基層 GROUND STOREY PLAN

The multi-eaved type is characterized by a high principal story, usually without a base, and with many courses of eaves, or cornices, above. The eaves are usually odd in number, seldom fewer than five and rarely exceeding thirteen. The combined height of the eaves is usually about twice that of the principal story. Because it is customary in China to designate the number of stories in a pagoda by the number of eaves, this type of pagoda is called "so-many-*storied*," which is misleading. Structurally, or architecturally, the eaves of this type are superposed directly one above another, with hardly any intermediate space. Therefore we shall use the designation "multi-eaved pagoda."

A masterpiece, although anything but typical, is the Pagoda of Sung-yueh Ssu, Teng-feng, in the Sung Mountains, Honan Province, built in 520. Indeed, it is a unique structure with its fifteen courses of eaves and twelve-sided plan. The general parti consists of an unusually high base, on which is elevated the principal story. This is decorated at each corner with an engaged column topped by a lotus-bud capital, a motif of Indian origin. Every side except the four that open with an arched doorway is treated with a niche containing a relief of a one-storied pagoda on a "lion pedestal." The courses of eaves diminish in a gentle parabolic curve, presenting an unusually graceful silhouette. The entire structure is a hollow shell of brick masonry, octagonal on the interior (figs. 66a, b). Because the original wooden floors and stairs have vanished the interior appears not unlike that of an elevator shaft.

The typical multi-eaved pagodas of this period are all square in plan and stand directly on the ground; the principal story is generally plain, without any decoration. The Pagodas of Yung-t'ai Ssu and of Fa-wang Ssu, both early eighth century and both in the Sung Mountains, Teng-feng, Honan Province, are the best examples (figs. 66c, d).

The Hsiao-yen T'a (684) of Chien-fu Ssu, Sian, Shensi Province, is a pagoda of this type but with windows on the narrow bands of wall separating the eaves (figs. 66e, f). The eaves, however, especially the higher ones, do not correspond with the floors and therefore do not express the interior divisions. The difference in height between the principal story and those of the upper "stories" is so marked, in contrast to the more regular progression of stories of the multi-storied type, that the pagoda must properly be classified as multi-eaved. The Pagoda of Fo-t'u Ssu (820?) and the Ch'ien-hsun T'a (ca. 850), both in Tali, Yunnan Province, are also multi-eaved (figs. 66g–j).

A number of stone pagodas of the T'ang dynasty belong to the multi-eaved type. They are usually small structures, rarely more than twenty-five or thirty feet high. The eaves are rather thin slabs carved into steps in imitation of the corbelled courses of the brick pagoda. The doorway on the principal story is usually carved as an arch with a flame-shaped archivolt and is flanked by two *dvrapalas* or guardian kings. Typical examples are the four stone pagodas of Yun-chu Ssu (711–722), Fang-shan, Hopei Province, which stand on the four corners of a large terrace as satellites to a large, later pagoda in the center (figs. 66k, l). This grouping of five pagodas on a common base will become quite usual in the Ming and Ch'ing dynasties.

b
Sung-yueh Ssu T'a, Teng-feng,
Sung Shan, Honan, 520.

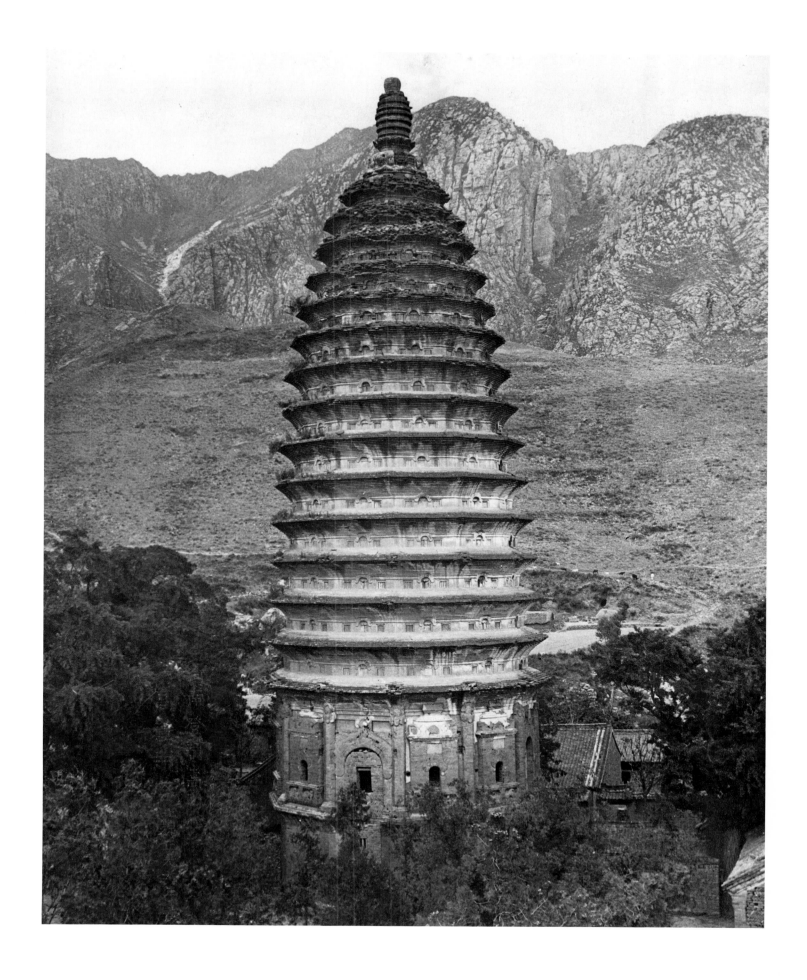

The Stupa

At about the end of the tenth century there appeared the stupa, a pagoda type that is more Indian than any we have seen. Tombs, in the form of Indian stupas with nearly hemispherical bodies, are frequently depicted in the mural paintings in the Tun-huang caves. Actual specimens of this date, however, though by no means rare in Chinese Turkestan, are very uncommon in China proper. One example is the Stupa at Fo-kuang Ssu. The stupa type eventually established a strong foothold in China and is discussed below under the Period of Variety.

66
Multi-eaved Pagodas
c
Yung-t'ai Ssu T'a, Teng-feng,
Honan, eighth century
d
Fa-wang Ssu T'a, Teng-feng,
Honan, eighth century

g
Fo-t'u Ssu T'a, Tali, Yunnan,
820(?)
h
Fo-t'u Ssu T'a, plan

e
Hsiao-yen T'a, Chien-fu Ssu,
Sian, Shensi, 684
f
Hsiao-yen T'a, plan

西安薦福寺小雁塔平面

雲南大理縣 佛圖寺塔 平面

66
Multi-eaved Pagodas
i
Ch'ien-hsun T'a, Tali, Yunnan,
ca. 850

PLOT PLAN
PAGODA GROUP
CH'UNG-SHENG SSU
TA-LI · YUNNAN

PRINCIPAL PAGODA: 9TH CENTURY
TWIN PAGODAS: 10TH-13TH CENTURIES

SOUTH PAGODA

NORTH PAGODA

千尋塔

TS'IEN-HSÜN T'A

雲南 大理縣
崇聖寺 三塔
總平面圖

主塔：南詔時(中晚唐)建
双塔：大理時(五代宋元)建

公尺 10   0   30m.

j
Ch'ien-hsun T'a and twin
pagodas, Tali, site plan

k
Stone Pagodas of Yun-chu Ssu,
Fang Shan, Hopei, showing two
of four small T'ang pagodas
(711–722) and base of large
central pagoda, a Liao
substitution

l
Detail of a small T'ang pagoda,
Yun-chu Ssu, Fang Shan

The Period of Elaboration (ca. 1000–1300)

The Period of Elaboration may be tentatively set from the end of the tenth to the end of the thirteenth centuries, that is, covering the Five Dynasties and the Northern and Southern Sung dynasties, as well as the Liao and Chin dynasties. The pagoda of this period is characterized by an octagonal plan and by the introduction of both horizontal and vertical masonry interior divisions in the form of galleries and built-in stairs. These divisions are a wide departure from the old hollow shell and give an entirely changed aspect to the interior. But the idea is not new, for it had already appeared once in the middle of the sixth century, in the Ssu-men T'a of Shen-t'ung Ssu (fig. 64a).

The octagonal pagoda which first appeared in the Tomb Pagoda of Ching-tsang in 746 (figs. 64d, e) was the first "pa-go-da" in the real sense of the term. The origin of this peculiar word has always been a mystery. Perhaps the most plausible explanation is that it is simply the southern pronunciation of the three characters *pa-chiao-t'a*—"pa-ko-t'a," meaning "eight-cornered pagoda." The word "pagoda" instead of "*t'a*" is deliberately used in this book because it is accepted in all the European languages as the name for such a monument. The very fact that the word finds its way into almost every European dictionary as the name for the Chinese *t'a* may refleet the popularity of the octagonal plan at the opening of Western contact.

The external aspect of the pagoda of this period is characterized by the ever-more faithful imitation of timber construction. Columns, architraves, elaborate and complicated sets of *tou-kung*, eaves with rafters, doors, windows, balconies with railings, and the like all make their appearance on the brick pagoda. Thus the multi-storied and multi-eaved pagodas of this period look quite different from their earlier prototypes.

One-storied Pagodas

The one-storied pagoda, which was very popular in the Period of Simplicity, became a rarity after the end of the T'ang dynasty. The few that remain from the twelfth century are still square in plan. The shrinelike pagoda is raised on a base of *shu-mi-tso*, a treatment not found in the T'ang dynasty examples. The entrance, which opened into the cella in the previous period, is now closed with doors, on which appear rows of "nail-heads" and knockers. Typical examples are the tombs of P'u-t'ung (1121), of Hsing-chun (926) (fig. 64f), and of Hsi-t'ang (1167), all in the Shao-lin Ssu in the Sung Mountains, Honan Province.

Multi-storied Pagodas

67

Multi-storied Pagodas of the
Timber-frame Subtype, North
China

a

Ch'ien-fo T'a, I Hsien, Hopei

As the one-storied pagoda gradually disappeared, changes also took place in the taller structures. The octagonal plan became the norm, the square plan the exception. The wooden floors and stairs that used to divide and connect the stories gave way to masonry floors and stairs. The architects were timid at first: the pagodas were built almost as solid masonry, bored through with narrow "tunnels" for galleries and stairways. As the builders gained in experience and audacity, the masonry was increasingly lightened by enlarging the galleries on each floor, until the structure became virtually a brick-masonry core with a semidetached shell. The two were bonded at intervals by arched or corbelled floors.

The multi-storied pagodas of this period may be divided into two subtypes: the "timber-frame subtype" and the "astylar subtype." The former may further be subdivided into the Liao or northern style, and the Sung or southern style.

The Liao timber-frame subtype may best be described as the rendition in brick of such structures as the Wooden Pagoda (1056) of Fo-kung Ssu, Ying Hsien, Shansi Province (fig. 31), which is the only surviving wooden pagoda in China. There are typical examples in Hopei Province—the Twin Pagodas of Yun-chu Ssu, Cho Hsien, built in 1090 (figs. 67b, c), and the Ch'ien-fo T'a of I Hsien (fig. 67a)—and a few similar structures in the provinces of Jehol and Liaoning. Their faithful adherence to the wooden form is obvious. The only difference in proportion is the narrow overhang of the eaves, due to the limitations of the material.

A pagoda belonging to the timber-frame subtype, but unique among all the pagodas in China, is the Hua T'a, or Flowery Pagoda of Kuang-hui Ssu, Cheng-ting, Hopei Province, so called because of its flowery appearance (figs. 67d, e). An octagonal brick structure of very fanciful plan and startling mass composition, it is treated with timber-frame forms on the exterior and surmounted by a colonial "spire" profusely decorated with the most fantastic motifs. Four hexagonal one-storied pagodas are attached to four sides of the ground story. This peculiar plan is probably a modified version of the arrangement of the Pagoda Group of Yun-chu Ssu, Fang-shan. The exact date of the Flowery Pagoda is unknown, but, judging by the stylistic characteristics of the timber construction imitated, it is probably of the late twelfth or early thirteenth century.

An unusual structure in the northern timber-frame subtype is the Pei T'a, or North Pagoda (fig. 67f), the central feature of the Yun-chu Ssu group, which stands amid the four earlier stone pagodas of T'ang date. This pagoda is only two stories high, apparently an unfinished structure of the Ying Hsien Wooden Pagoda type. It is surmounted by a large stupa with a hemispherical "belly" and a large conical "neck." The lower two stories are undoubtedly of the Liao dynasty; the upper part may be later.

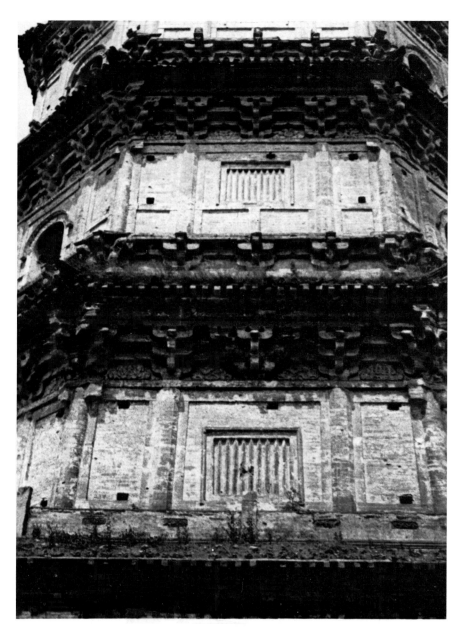

67
Multi-storied Pagodas of the
Timber-frame Subtype, North
China
b
Detail of North Pagoda, Yun-
chu Ssu, Cho Hsien
c
North Pagoda of the Twin
Pagodas of Yun-chu Ssu, Cho
Hsien, Hopei, 1090

d
Hua T'a (Flowery Pagoda),
Kuang-hui Ssu, Cheng-ting,
Hopei, ca. 1200. (Destroyed)
e
Hua T'a, plan
f
Pei T'a (North Pagoda), Yun-
chu Ssu, Fang Shan, Hopei,
Liao dynasty

河北正定縣廣惠寺華塔平面圖

公尺 5　0　　　　10M.

The southern Sung timber-frame subtype is quite common in the lower Yangtze region. The earliest examples are three small stone pagodas located in Hangchow, Chekiang Province. These miniature pagodas (about thirty feet tall), which are really Dhanari columns in pagoda form, are carved with great dexterity and are no doubt very faithful copies of wooden structures of the time. Two examples are the Twin Pagodas (960) in front of the Main Hall of Ling-yin Ssu (figs. 68a, b), and the third is the Pai T'a in the railroad yard at the Cha-k'ou Station.

However, true pagodas typical of this southern style are exemplified in the Twin Pagodas of Lo-han Yuan (982), Soochow, Kiangsu Province, and the Tiger Hill Pagoda in the same city (figs. 68c–g). Compared to their northern counterparts they are characterized by a marked slenderness in general proportion, which is further emphasized by the tall, slim metal *sha*, or spire, and the absence of the high *shu-mi-tso* base. In detail the columns are shorter but of more delicate entasis. The *tou-kung* are simpler, due to the absence of the diagonal *kung* and to the "stolen heart" on the first "jump." The rafters are merely suggested by the chevron courses, called *ling-chiao ya-tzu*, in the narrow corbelled cornice. Thus the eave overhang is very slight, giving the pagoda a silhouette entirely different from that of the northern structures.

The two ashlar pagodas at Chin-chiang (Ch'uan-chou), Fukien Province, the Chen-kuo T'a and the Jen-shou T'a (1228–1247), are stone versions of the southern timber-frame subtype. Their affinity to the wooden form is obvious. Because almost all masonry pagodas are brick structures, these two examples in stone are valuable rarities.

The astylar subtype, that is, the structures that are not treated with columns on the facade, is primarily a Northern Sung product. Existing specimens are mostly found in the provinces of Honan, Hopei, and Shantung, and less commonly in other parts of China. These pagodas are characterized by the complete absence of columns or pilasters on the walls. The *tou-kung*, however, is often used; there are a number of examples with cornices built up by corbelled courses of brick. The *tou-kung* may not necessarily appear in distinct separate sets, but they are often arranged in a row, producing a band of vibrating light and shade under the eave. In most cases the architrave is shown above the wall to receive the *tou-kung*.

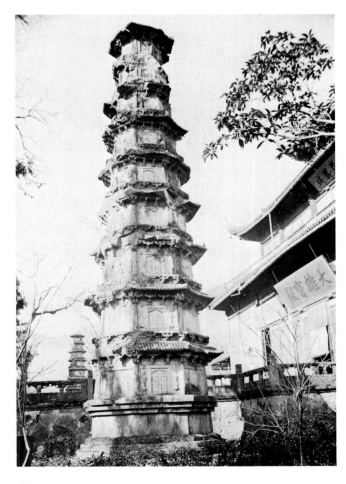

68
Multi-storied Pagodas of the
Timber-frame Subtype, South
China

a
Twin Pagodas, Ling-yin Ssu,
Hangchow, Chekiang, 960

b
Detail of one Twin Pagoda,
Ling-yin Ssu
c
Twin Pagodas, Lo-han Yuan,
Soochow, Kiangsu, 982,
rendering.

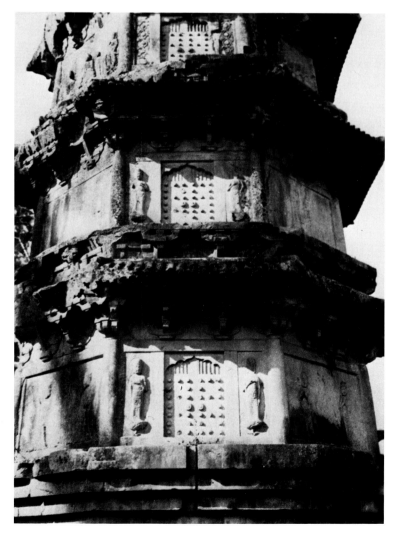

68
Multi-storied Pagodas of the
Timber-frame Subtype, South
China
d
Twin Pagodas, Lo-han Yuan,
plans, section, and details
e
Detail of one Twin Pagoda,
Lo-han Yuan

西塔内部第一層斷面畵
SECTION, 1ST FLOOR, WEST PAGODA

西塔第二層立面詳畵
DETAIL OF EXTERIOR, 2ND FLOOR, WEST PAGODA

西塔第二層外層斷面

'8尺 50　0　　　1　　　2M.
詳畵縮尺　SCALE FOR DETAILS

北

宋太平興國七年建
SUNG DYNASTY, 982 A.D.

雙塔平面畵
PLAN OF TWIN-PAGODAS

江蘇吳縣 羅漢院雙塔
TWIN PAGODAS, SOOCHOW, CHIANGSU

'8尺 1　0　　　　5　　　　10 METRES
平面縮尺　SCALE FOR PLAN

Tiger Hill Pagoda, Soochow,
Kiangsu
g
Detail of Tiger Hill Pagoda

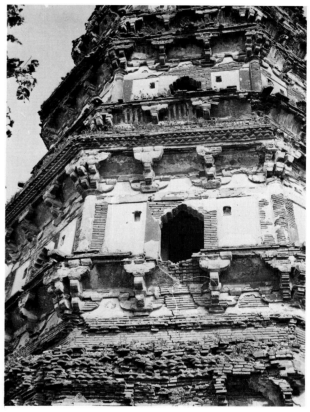

Typical of this subtype with *tou-kung* treatment are the P'i-chih T'a of Ling-yen Ssu (fig. 69a), Ch'ang-ch'ing, Shantung Province, and the Pagoda of Shen-kuo Ssu, Hsiu-wu, Honan Province, both of the late eleventh century. An excellent example of the corbelled eave kind is the Liao-ti T'a of K'ai-yuan Ssu (1001), Ting Hsien, Hopei Province (fig. 69b). The northwest section of this structure has completely fallen off, exposing the internal construction like a model of a cross section made especially for the convenience of the student of Chinese architecture (fig. 69c). Pagodas of this kind are also found in the southwest, such as the Pai T'a of Pao-en Ssu (ca. 1155), Ta-chu, and another at Lu Hsien, both in the province of Szechuan.

The Sung dynasty introduced the use of terra-cotta as facing for pagodas. The so-called "Iron Pagoda" of Yu-kuo Ssu (1041), K'aifeng, Honan Province, is a notable northern example (figs. 69d, e). The structure is a multi-storied pagoda with a very slight indication of columns at the corners, and is faced with terra-cotta tiles. Glazed in brown, they produce an effect like that of oxidized iron, from which the structure got its popular name.

Pagodas actually made of iron are, however, not uncommon in the Sung dynasty. They are usually small and very slender because of the nature of the material—cast iron. Like the stone pagodas of Hangchow, these miniature pagodas are really Dhanari columns in the form of pagodas. Examples are found in the Yu-ch'uan Ssu, Tang-yang, Hupei Province, and in Tsi-ning, Shantung Province.

69
Multi-storied Pagodas of the
Astylar Subtype
a
P'i-chih T'a, Ling-yen Ssu,
Ch'ang-ch'ing, Shantung, late
eleventh century
b
Liao-ti T'a, K'ai-yuan Ssu, Ting
Hsien, Hopei, 1001
c
Northwest side of Liao-ti T'a

d
The "Iron Pagoda," Yu-kuo
Ssu, K'aifeng, Honan, 1041
e
"Iron Pagoda," plan

河南開封市祐國寺鉄塔平面圖

Multi-eaved Pagodas

70

Multi-eaved Pagodas

a

T'ien-ning Ssu T'a, Peking, eleventh century

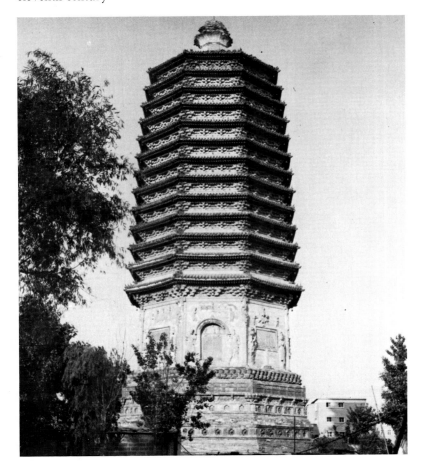

After the fall of the T'ang dynasty the multi-eaved pagoda became almost exclusively an expression of the Liao and Chin Tartars. It is the type commonly seen in North China today. Treated with timber forms, it now presents an aspect quite different from its predecessors in the Period of Simplicity. The octagonal plan, with a few rare exceptions, is universally adopted. But the structure has become a solid pile of masonry, no longer to be entered and ascended. The whole structure is invariably raised on a high *shu-mi-tso* base, which in turn is sometimes elevated on a broad, low platform. The principal story is treated with engaged columns at the corners, architraves, and blind doors and windows on the walls. The successive tiers of eaves are usually supported by *tou-kung*, accurately rendered in brick. But the corbelled eave is also common, and sometimes both treatments are combined in one pagoda by limiting the *tou-kung* to the lowest eave only.

A typical example is the well-known Pagoda of T'ien-ning Ssu, Peking (fig. 70a). Above the *shu-mi-tso* a *p'ing-tso* of lotus petals further elevates the structure. The doors are flanked by guardian kings, and the windows by standing Bodhisattvas. The building is of the eleventh century but somewhat freely repaired in later periods.

A good example with corbelled upper eaves is the Pagoda of T'ai-ning Ssu, I Hsien, Hopei Province. The Ch'ing T'a of Lin-chi Ssu (1185), Cheng-ting, Hopei Province, is a smaller structure of the same type. The Tomb Pagoda of Chen-chi, Po-lin Ssu (1228), Chao Hsien, Hopei Province, is a similar structure with a slight modification, the indication of a very low story under each of the upper eaves (fig. 70b). This departure from the norm may be considered a compromise between the multi-eaved and multi-storied types.

Occasionally multi-eaved pagodas of this period still cling to the traditions of the Period of Simplicity, such as the square plan. A good example is the Ta T'a, or Big Pagoda, of Feng-huang Shan, Ch'ao-yang, Liaoning Province, probably of the thirteenth century. The Pagoda of Pai-ma Ssu, near Loyang, Honan Province, built in 1175 when that region was under the Chin Tartars, is a square pagoda with thirteen tiers of cornices (fig. 70c). The plan and the general proportions are obviously in the T'ang manner. But the structure is a solid and is raised on a *shu-mi-tso*—both characteristics not found in the previous period.

Another example, the Pai T'a of I-pin, Szechuan Province, ca. 1102–1109, is absolutely T'ang in character if judged only by its appearance (fig. 70d). But the interior arrangement, with a cella in the core, surrounded by a continuous gallery and stairs, is characteristic of its own time.

Square pagodas of the T'ang style are quite numerous in the southwestern provinces, especially in Yunnan where they were built in the old manner as late as the Ch'ing dynasty.

b
Tomb Pagoda of Chen-chi,
Po-lin Ssu, Chao Hsien, Hopei,
1228
c
Pai-ma Ssu T'a, near Loyang,
Honan, 1175
d
Pai T'a, I-pin, Szechuan, ca.
1102–1109, plan and elevation

四川宜賓縣舊州壩白塔　宋崇寧大觀間建

前面立面圖 FRONT ELEVATION

下層平面圖 GROUND FLOOR PLAN

PAGODA AT CHIU-CHOU-PA,
YI-PIN, SZECHUAN
SUNG DYNASTY, 1102-09 A.D.

Dhanari Columns

One peculiar Buddhist monument that originated some time in the T'ang dynasty and became very popular in the Period of Elaboration is the *ching-chuang*, or Dhanari column, which is also called *ching-t'a*, or Dhanari pagoda. The distinction depends upon the similarity of the edifice to a real pagoda. These monuments vary widely in "architecturesqueness," from a simple octagonal column set on a *shu-mi-tso* base and crowned by a sort of cornice or umbrella, to the shape of a real pagoda, though always much smaller.

The Dhanari column in front of the Main Hall of Fo-kuang Ssu, dated 857 and bearing the name of Ning Kung-yu, donor of the Hall, is a typical simple example (fig. 71a). The column in Feng-ch'ung Ssu, Hsing-t'ang, Hopei Province, probably of the twelfth century, is characteristic of numerous *ching-chuang* of the Sung and Chin dynasties. The *ching-chuang* of Chao Hsien, Hopei Province, highly elaborate in treatment and very graceful in proportions, is the largest of its kind known (fig. 71b). It is also attributed to the early Sung dynasty, probably the eleventh century. Another interesting specimen is the thirteenth-century Dhanari column of Ti-tsang An, Kunming, Yunnan Province. The whole is conceived more as a piece of sculpture than architecture. Monuments of this kind seem to have lost their popularity with the fall of the Sung dynasty.

71
Dhanari Columns
a
Dhanari column,
Fo-kuang Ssu, 857

山西 五台山 佛光寺
晚 唐 兩 經 幢
TWO DHANARI COLUMNS
OF THE LATE T'ANG PERIOD
FO-KUANG SSU
WU-T'AI SHAN · SHANSI

圓 Round

圓 Round

八 角 Octagonal

大中十一年幢

乾符四年幢

八 角 Octagonal

圓 Round
八 角 Octagonal

圓 Round
八 角 Octagonal

857 A.D.

887 A.D.

公分 50   0   100 cm.

Dhanari column, Chao Hsien,
Hopei, early Sung dynasty

The Period of Variety (ca. 1280–1912)

We shall call the period from the founding of the Yuan dynasty in 1279 to the fall of the Ch'ing dynasty in 1912 the Period of Variety. Its first innovation was the sudden popularity of the "bottle-shaped" pagoda (the Tibetan version of the Indian stupa), which followed the introduction of the Lamaist sect of Buddhism by the conquering Mongols. This type had been faintly heralded about three centuries earlier in the Stupa of Fo-kuang Ssu. In the Chin dynasty it had been adopted in various modified forms as a tomb monument for monks. Finally it became firmly established in the Yuan dynasty.

The second innovation was the formulation in the Ming dynasty of the *chin-kang pao-tso t'a*, or the clustering of five pagodas on a common high terrace. Again, this arrangement had already been suggested in the five pagodas of Yun-chu Ssu of Fang Shan, Hopei (fig. 66k), in the early eighth century. But it lay dormant for more than seven hundred years, until the latter part of the fifteenth century. Though it never became popular enough to be found throughout China, the existing examples constitute a definite type.

Large numbers of the more conventional types of pagoda were built in the Ming and Ch'ing dynasties, not always at the service of Buddhism. They were often erected as devices for the control or rectification of certain defects in *feng-shui* (literally, "wind and water"), a geomancy based on the influence over human destinies of the elements of nature, especially topographical peculiarities and orientation. A common expression of this belief is the *wen-fang t'a*, the tower that brings good luck to those taking literary examinations. They are seen throughout southern China, where they are usually erected on an elevated terrain to the south or southeast of many a walled town.

Multi-storied Pagodas

With the end of the Chin dynasty in 1234, the multi-eaved pagoda suddenly fell out of popularity, and the multi-storied pagoda became the dominant type. Its outstanding characteristics during the Ming dynasty were its increased slenderness and its squatter division of stories. The general contour shows less entasis and, in some cases, more tapering in a harsh straight line. The eaves became mere rings, with a narrow overhang and very flimsy *tou-kung* (if used at all), reflecting their diminished proportion in the wooden originals of the day. Examples of this type are numerous. The Pagoda of Ching-yang, Shensi Province, an early-sixteenth-century structure, is quite reminiscent of the Period of Elaboration. The pagoda of Ling-yen Ssu, Fen-yang, Shansi Province, built in 1549, is a most typical Ming pagoda. The Twin Pagodas of Yung-chao Ssu (fig. 72a), Taiyuan, Shansi Province, built in 1595, have a comparatively greater overhang of the eaves, which cast deeper shadows for a more accentuated appearance than is normally found in pagodas of the Ming dynasty.

The Fei-hung T'a of Kuang-sheng Ssu, Chao-ch'eng, Shansi Province, built in 1515, is a peculiar example (fig. 72b). The thirteen stories diminish in a strong taper, without the slightest entasis, presenting the appearance of an awkwardly proportioned octagonal pyramid. The awkwardness is emphasized by the addition of an excessively wide timber gallery around the ground story. The exterior is burdened by a profusion of ornaments in yellow and green glazed terra-cotta, while *tou-kung* and lotus petals are employed as supports for the eaves of alternate stories. In construction the building is virtually a solid pile of masonry, bored through by a zigzag stairway tunnel that is most ingeniously constructed for the total elimination of landings (fig. 72c).

A monument of more or less the same category, and equally distasteful in appearance, is the square pagoda of Ta-yun Ssu, Lin-fen, Shansi Province, built in 1651 (fig. 72d). The five-story square structure is surmounted by an octagonal "lantern," which is a most novel way of interpreting the *sha*. In the ground-story cella is a colossal head of Buddha, about twenty feet high, resting directly on the ground. This iconographic treatment is itself as unorthodox as the design of the pagoda that houses it.

A few other multi-storied pagodas of the Ch'ing dynasty may be mentioned. The Pagoda of Hsin-chiang, Shansi Province, is of the astylar subtype. Though adhering much to the tradition of the last period, it is characterized by entasis which is carried too high, resulting in a spikelike contour. The Pagoda of Feng-sheng Ssu, Chin-tz'u, near T'ai-yuan, Shansi Province, is of the northern timber-frame subtype, with a pleasing appearance not unlike that of the Liao structures (fig. 72e). The Pei T'a, or North Pagoda, of Chin-hua, Chekiang Province, is a representative southern example (fig. 72f).

72
Period of Variety: Multi-storied
Pagodas
a
Twin Pagodas, Yung-chao
Ssu, Taiyuan, Shansi, 1595

72
Period of Variety: Multi-storied
pagodas
b
Fei-hung T'a, Kuang-sheng Ssu,
Chao-ch'eng, Shansi, 1515
c
Fei-hung T'a, section through
stairway

d
Square Pagoda, Ta-yun Ssu,
Lin-fen, Shansi, 1651
e
Feng-sheng Ssu T'a, Chin-tz'u,
Taiyuan, Shansi
f
Pei T'a, Chin-hua, Chekiang,
Ch'ing dynasty

Multi-eaved Pagodas

With the fall of the Chin dynasty, construction of multi-eaved pagodas virtually ceased. Besides the two pairs of Twin Pagodas in Peking, which are rather small and were originally Yuan structures but almost completely rebuilt during the Ch'ing dynasty, the only "full-size" multi-eaved pagoda we know from the Yuan dynasty is the one at T'ien-ning Ssu, Anyang, Honan Province (fig. 73a). This structure as it now stands, with its five decks of eaves or stories, is evidently unfinished, like so many of the towers of Gothic cathedrals in France. Like the tomb Pagoda of Chen-chi, Po-lin Ssu, Chao Hsien, Hopei Province (fig. 70b), there is a very low story under each tier of eaves. Therefore, it is not even multi-eaved in the strict sense, but appears so only in general effect. It is terminated by a *sha* in the form of a stupa typical of the Ch'ing style. The timber-form details represented on the facades of the principal story reflect very faithfully the wooden construction of the day. The pagoda is unusual in plan as well as in exterior appearance, for it is not solid like similar structures of the Liao and Chin dynasties. Except for the ground story, which has a stairway around the cella, the whole is a hollow shell like the T'ang pagodas. This plan is rarely seen in later ages.

Though no longer favored as a full-size edifice, the multi-eaved pagoda became quite popular as a tomb monument in the Yuan dynasty. Two excellent small examples are the Tomb Pagoda of Hung-tz'u Po-hua Ta-shih and the Tomb Pagoda of Hsu-chao (ca. 1290), both in Hsing-t'ai, Hopei Province. The latter is hexagonal in plan and is surmounted by a hemispherical stupa (fig. 73b). In the southwestern province of Yunnan, where the influence of the cultural centers was slow to permeate, the multi-eaved pagoda was still built under the Mongols, but usually in the T'ang style with a square plan and corbelled cornices.

The only multi-eaved pagoda of the Ming dynasty is the Tz'u-shou Ssu Pagoda at Pa-li-chuang, Peking (fig. 73c). Built in 1578, it was unquestionably inspired by the nearby T'ien-ning Ssu Pagoda (fig. 70a), whose general proportion it follows closely. But in detail it shows all the traits of the late Ming dynasty, such as the slight projection of the moldings of the *shu-mi-tso*, the comparatively low main story, the arched windows, the double architrave, and the small *tou-kung*.

A small pagoda, erected as a garden feature in the Yu-ch'uan Shan (Jade Fountain Park) near Peking in the eighteenth century, shows an interesting innovation of the Ch'ing dynasty. It may be considered a combination of the multi-storied and multi-eaved types. Of its three stories, the lower two are double-eaved, while the top story is triple-eaved, presenting a not unpleasant effect. The plan, though octagonal, is not equilateral, and it may be better described as a square with splayed corners. The whole structure is faced with glazed terra-cotta, and timber construction is very faithfully imitated on the facades.

73
Period of Variety: Multi-eaved
Pagodas
a
Tz'u-shou Ssu T'a,
Pa–li–chuang, Peking, 1578.

73
Period of Variety: Multi-eaved
Pagodas
b
Tomb Pagoda of Hsu-chao,
Hsing-t'ai, Hopei, ca. 1290
c
Tz'u-shou Ssu T'a,
Pa-li-chuang, Peking, 1578.
Another view

As we have seen, the Lamaist stupa was heralded in the hemispherical tomb in Fo-kuang Ssu in the latter part of the tenth century and was adopted in certain tomb features in the Chin dynasty, but it did not formally appear as a monumental edifice until the Yuan dynasty. Its appearance assumed a new form: a bottle-shaped super-structure on a high base. The base is usually a *shu-mi-tso* of one or two tiers, the plan of which we shall call, for want of a better name, a square with "folded-in corners," or with projections on the four sides. The "bottle" consists of a "belly" and a "neck," which is often crowned by an "umbrella".

The prototype is the Pai T'a of Miao-ying Ssu, Peking (fig. 74a). It was built in 1271 by order of Kublai Khan, who deliberately had the existing Liao pagoda destroyed in order to replace it with the present structure. It is distinguished from later pagodas of its type by its sturdy proportions, the almost vertical sides of its "belly," and the truncated-cone "bottle-neck."

The outstanding bottle-shaped pagoda of the Ming dynasty is the Pagoda of T'a-yuan Ssu (1577), in the Wu-t'ai Mountains, Shansi Province (fig. 74b). Here the bottom of the "bottle" is slightly diminished, while the top of the "neck" is enlarged. The general aspect is more slender than that of the Pai T'a of Peking.

A stupa of the Ming dynasty, whose exact date is uncertain, is the Pagoda of Shan-kuo Ssu, Tai Hsien, Shansi Province. The *shu-mi-tso* base, with its simple, bold moldings, is circular in plan and much larger than usual in proportion to the superstructure. The recession of the upper tier of *shu-mi-tso* is greater than usual. The "belly" has a soft, gentle contour, while the "neck" is pinched around its bottom as it rises from its own *shu-mi-tso* base. The general effect is one of steadiness and elegance, and the stupa may be considered the best proportioned bottle-shaped pagoda in China.

In time the Lamaist stupa became more slender, especially in the "neck." Two typical examples are the Pai T'a of Yung-an Ssu (1651) in the Pei Hai (North Lake) Park, Peking (fig. 74c), and the stupa surmounting the archway at the entrance to the ruined site of Fa-hai Ssu (1660), near the Hunting Park, Ching-yi Yuan, in the Western Hills, Peking. The two structures, though differing greatly in size, are almost identical in general proportion. In both, the high *shu-mi-tso* base is simplified to only one tier. The moldings above the *shu-mi-tso* and around the bottom of the "bottle," which formerly presented the cross section of a cyma, have now become taller, and at Fa-hai Ssu, they have become an additional stepped base, following the profile of the *shu-mi-tso* base below. The niche on the "belly," has now become a standardized feature. The "neck" has become almost cylindrical, with only a slight tapering, and is very slender in proportion to the "belly."

A few monuments of the same type are found in the neighborhood of Shenyang (Mukden), Liaoning Province, relics of the early Ch'ing dynasty. They are distinguished by their very large "bellies" and broad bases. Various modifications of this type, usually small and executed in bronze, are used as ornamental features in temple grounds. Those in front of the Main Hall of Hsien-ch'ing Ssu in the Wu-t'ai Mountains, Shansi Province, are typical.

74

Period of Variety: Lamaist
Stupas

a

Pai T'a, Miao-ying Ssu, Peking,
1271

b

T'a-yuan Ssu T'a, Wu-t'ai Shan,
Shansi, 1577

c

Pai T'a, Yung-an Ssu, Pei Hai
(North Lake) Park, Peking,
1651

Five-pagoda Clusters

The one important contribution of the Ming dynasty to the art of pagoda building is the definite formulation of the *chin-kang pao-tso t'a*, or the "Vajra-based pagoda," the grouping of five pagodas on a common base. We have seen the first suggestion of such an arrangement in the Yun-chu Ssu group of 711–722 (fig. 66k). In the middle of the T'ang dynasty (late eighth century), a more exuberant manifestation appears in the Pagoda of Ch'iu-t'a Ssu near Ch'ang-ch'ing, Shantung Province, where nine small square multieaved pagodas are clustered on top of an octagonal one-storied pagoda. In the Chin dynasty the idea takes a curious form in the Flowery Pagoda of Cheng-ting (fig. 67d). However, it was not until the T'ien-chun period (1457–1460) of the Ming dynasty, with the erection of the Chin-kang Pao-tso T'a at Miao-chan Ssu, near Kun-ming, Yunnan Province, that the type was definitely formed. This group is composed of five Lamaist stupas on a common terrace or base. The slender "neck," refined by a slight entasis, is unusual for the stupa type, while the niche in the "belly" is unusual for this early date. The terrace is penetrated by two intersecting barrel vaults, but no access is provided for ascending it.

The most important five-pagoda cluster is the Chin-kang Pao-tso T'a of Cheng-chueh Ssu, popularly known as the Wu-t'a Ssu, or Five-Pagoda Temple, outside the west wall of Peking (fig. 75a). It was built in 1473. The monumental is divided into five stories and treated with continuous rows of cornices, suggestive of a Tibetan temple building. The south facade is penetrated by an archway that opens onto the stairway leading to the top of the terrace. The pagodas themselves are of the square, multi-eaved type. A pavilion is placed in the center on the front of the terrace, forming a "penthouse" that covers the upper entrance of the stairway.

Another important example of this type is the Chin-kang Pao-tso T'a of Pi-yun Ssu, in the Western Hills, Peking (figs. 75b, c). In this group, erected in 1747, the arrangement of the Wu-t'a Ssu group has been further elaborated. Two additional bottle-shaped stupas are placed in front of the five square, multi-eaved pagodas. The pavilion in front, here standing between and behind the two stupas, is itself a smaller terrace, upon which the same theme of the five pagodas is repeated. The whole ensemble is further elevated by the two tiers of high terraces of rubble stone masonry on which it rests.

The group in the Yellow Temple, also of the eighteenth century, outside the north wall of Peking, is much smaller in scale. The Lamaist stupa in the center is fantastic in shape, while the four corner pagodas are octagonal and multi-storied. The group is placed on a low base on a low platform and preceded by a *p'ai-lou*.

75
Period of Variety: Five-pagoda Clusters
a
Wu T'a Ssu (Five-pagoda Temple), Cheng-chueh Ssu, Peking, 1473
b
Chin-kang Pao-tso T'a, Pi-yun Ssu, Peking, 1747
c
Pi-yun Ssu, plan and elevation

前面立面　FRONT ELEVATION

平面圖　PLAN

平面縮尺　SCALE FOR PLAN

北平西山碧雲寺金剛寶座塔

清乾隆十三年建

CHIN-KANG-PAO-TSO T'A
PI-YÜN SSU, WESTERN HILLS,
PEIPING.　CH'ING DYNASTY, 1748.

斷面縮尺　SCALE FOR SECTION

REDRAWN FROM BOERSCHMANN: CHINESISCHE ARCHITEKTUR.

Other Masonry Structures

The Chinese builder never cultivated a real knowledge of brick and stone as primary structural media for ordinary use. They were either reserved for structures that were not intimately involved with everyday life, such as city and garden walls, bridges, gateways, or tombs, or assigned to secondary functions, such as curtain walls or the walls coming up to the window sills of timber-framed buildings. Masonry structures, therefore, occupy a position in no sense comparable to that in European architecture.

Tombs

The oldest remains of vaulted construction are the brick tombs of the Han dynasty, which are found in great number. The subterranean structures are never architecturally treated and are thus of little architectural interest. Above ground the tomb or tumulus is usually preceded by an avenue, flanked at the entrance by a pair of *ch'üeh* (piers), then by figures of attendants, guards, and animals, and terminated by a shrine in front of the tumulus. The *ch'üeh* and the shrine are the only items of architectural interest, for the figures are of more importance to the student of sculpture than to the student of architecture. The tombs of the Six Dynasties and the T'ang dynasty are of even less interest to us, as all the remains are sculptural.

The incidental discovery of a few twelfth-century tombs in the neighborhood of I-pin and Nan-hsi, Szechuan Province, has revealed the high degree of architectural treatment of tombs of the Southern Sung dynasty. These small ashlar funeral chambers are given architectural elements that closely imitate wooden construction of the time. The end facing the entrance is invariably in the form of a pair of half-open doors from which emerges a female figure (fig. 76a). Similar tombs have not yet been found in other parts of China, so whether this is a purely local type or not is open to question.

There are many tombs from the Ming and Ch'ing dynasties, the most important of which are the imperial tombs. The aboveground structures are essentially temples, placed in front of the tumulus. It would be quite appropriate to call such groups "tomb temples." Their only important distinguishing feature is perhaps the *fang-ch'eng*, or "square bastion," surmounted by the *ming-lou*, or "radiant tower," which marks the entrance to the *ti-kung*, or "underground palace". The Tomb of the Ming emperor Yung-lo (figs. 76b, c), at Ch'ang-p'ing, is the most magnificent of the imperial tombs at Ch'ang-p'ing (Ming), I Hsien (Ch'ing), and Hsing-lung (Ch'ing), all in Hopei.

The Tomb of the Ch'ing emperor Chia-ch'ing (1820), at I Hsien, is a typical underground palace. From beneath the square bastion a passage leads to a series of gates, doors, passageways, antechambers, and finally to the "golden chamber," where the coffin of the emperor is laid. These "palaces" are vaulted, finished in marble, decorated with carvings, and generally roofed with yellow glazed tiles, exactly like a surface structure, though they were covered over with the ramped earth and lime-concrete that formed the tumulus. In some cases, however, they were not roofed, usually by will of the deceased emperor who wished to set an example of frugality. Drawings from the files, or rather from the wastepaper dumps, of the Lei family, hereditary architects to the imperial household of the Ch'ing dynasty for several hundred years, furnish interesting information about these "forbidden structures" (fig. 76d).

a
Unidentified tomb, I-pin,
Szechuan, ca. 1170

内部 INTERIOR VIEW

平面 PLAN

AN UNIDENTIFIED TOMB C.1170
I-PIN SZECHUAN

76
Tombs
b
Tomb of Ming emperor
Yung-lo, Ch'ang-p'ing, Hopei,
1415, showing "radiant tower"
(*ming-lou*) set on "square
bastion" (*fang-ch'eng*)
c
Yung-lo's tomb, plan

1 - 陵門 LING-MEN
    FORE GATE
2 - 碑亭 PEI-T'ING
    STELE PAVILLION
3 - 稜恩門 LING-ÊN MEN
    MAIN GATE
4 - 焚帛爐 FENG-PO-LU
    PAPER BURNERS
5 - 稜恩殿 LING-ÊN TIEN
    SACRIFICIA HALL
6 - 內紅門 NEI-HUNG-MEN
    INNER GATE
7 - 牌樓門 P'AI-LOU-MEN
    P'AI-LOU
8 - 五供桌 WU-KUNG-CHO
    INCENCE & CANDLES TABLE
9 - 方城 FANG-CH'ENG
    'SQUARE BASTION'
10 - 明樓 MING-LOU
    'RADIANT TOWER'
11 - 寶城 PAO-CH'ENG
    RETAINING WALL
12 - 寶頂 PAO-TING
    TUMULUS

PLOT PLAN

河北昌平縣 明長陵 總平面圖

明永樂七年至廿二年間建

自北平市工務局實測圖重摹

CH'ANG-LING · TOMB OF EMPEROR YUNG-LO
CH'ANG-P'ING · HOPEI ·· MING DYNASTY · 1409-24
REDRAWN AFTER PLAN BY THE BUREAU OF CONSTRUCTION · MUNICIPAL GOVERNMENT OF PEIPING

d

Tomb of Ch'ing emperor
Chia-ch'ing, I Hsien, Hopei,
1820, site plan and elevation.

清昌陵地宮斷面及平面圖（陵在河北省易縣）

自國立北平圖書館藏 樣式房雷氏圖重摹

| WALL | FILL (LIME AND EARTH) | "GOLDEN CHAMBER" | VAULTED PASSAGE | ANTI-CHAMBER | VAULTED DOORWAY | VAULTED PASSAGE | OPEN PASSAGE (FILLED & PAVED) | MING LOU "THE RADIANT TOWER" FANG CH'ENG "THE SQUARE BASTION" |

CH'ANG LING, TOMB OF EMPEROR CHIA-CH'ING, 1796-1820, CH'ING DYNASTY
PLAN AND SECTION OF SUBTERRANEAN TOMB CHAMBERS, REDRAWN AFTER ORIGINAL DRAWINGS
BY THE LEI FAMILY, HEREDITARY OFFICIAL ARCHITECTURAL DESIGNERS. (COLLECTION, NATIONAL PEIPING LIBRARY).

Vaulted Buildings

Except in the province of Shansi, the use of masonry for aboveground structures is extremely rare. A common type of house in Shansi is the vaulted house, which usually consists of three to seven barrel vaults placed side by side and parallel to each other. Penetrations cut as doorways allow circulation from vault to vault. The vaults are usually elliptical or parabolic in cross section, and the open ends are filled in with windows atop "window-sill walls." The spandrels are filled in to form a flat top, reached by an exterior stairway.

A vaulted building, called the *wu-liang tien* or "beamless hall," is occasionally used as the main hall in a temple. The temple of Yung-chao Ssu (1597), where the Twin Pagodas are also located, T'aiyuan, Shansi Province, is the best example (figs. 77a, b). Here the barrel vaulting runs lengthwise, with penetrations for doors and windows like those of ordinary Shansi dwellings. But the exterior is treated with columns, architraves, *tou-kung*, and other elements. Similar structures are also found in the Hsien-ch'ing Ssu, in the Wu-t'ai Mountains, Shansi Province, and at Soochow, Kiangsi Province (figs. 77c, d).

The practice of architecturally treating the exterior of a brick vaulted structure to resemble a conventional wood-frame main hall did not exist before the latter half of the Ming dynasty, though it had been common on pagodas. The treatment is analogous to the application of the classical orders in Renaissance buildings in Europe. It is interesting to note that with the arrival of Matteo Ricci at Nanking in 1587 and the beginning of Jesuit influence on Chinese culture, the vaulted buildings already existing in Shansi prepared a fertile ground. The proximity in date of the arrival of the Jesuits in China and the appearance of the *wu-liang tien* may not be entirely coincidental.

In the neighborhood of Peking are a few *wu-liang tien* of the Ch'ing dynasty (fig. 77e). Much larger than the Ming structures in Shansi, they are astylar in treatment. The "columns" are "hidden" in their massive walls: only the tops of the columns are indicated with architraves and *tou-kung*. These features are all in glazed terra-cotta. It is difficult to understand why these very impressive and monumental buildings were not more widely adopted.

77
Vaulted "beamless halls"
(*wu-liang tien*)
a
Yung-chao Ssu, T'aiyuan,
Shansi, 1597
b
Yung-chao Ssu, plan

山西太原永祚寺磚殿平面圖

YUNG-CHAO SSU, T'AI-YUAN, SHANSI, PLAN OF BRICK
VAULTED HALLS. 明萬曆二十五年建. A.D. 1597.

77
Vaulted "beamless halls"
c
K'ai-yuan Ssu, Soochow,
Kiangsi
d
K'ai-yuan Ssu, interior detail of
vaulting
e
Beamless hall, Western Hills,
Peking, eighteenth century

The earliest bridges in China were of wood, and pontoon bridges were used for crossing wide rivers. It was not until the fourth century A.D. that the first arched bridge was recorded in literature.

The oldest arched bridge in China today is the An-chi Ch'iao, popularly known as the Great Stone Bridge (figs. 78a, b), near Chao Hsien, Hopei Province. It is an open spandrel bridge with two smaller arches at each end of the principal arch, which is segmental. The bridge is 115 feet long between the points where the two ends now emerge from the banks of the river. The clear span, if excavated from the banks, would be considerably longer. But our attempts to find its spring line by excavation at the abutments failed when we reached the water level seven feet below the dry riverbed.

The bridge is the work of the master builder Li Ch'un of the Sui dynasty (581–618). The principal arch is composed of twenty-eight separate strings of arches, placed side by side. The builder was fully aware of the danger of the strings falling apart, as is evidenced by his narrowing the top of the bridge toward the crown to give an inward incline to the exterior arches, thus counteracting the eccentric tendency of the separate rings. However, his foresight and ingenuity did not succeed against time and the elements. Five rings on the west side fell off in the sixteenth century (restored not long afterward), and three on the east fell in the eighteenth century.

A smaller bridge of similar design stands outside the west gate of the same city, Chao Hsien, known as the Little Stone Bridge (fig. 78c). It was built by Pao Ch'ien-erh at the end of the twelfth century, undoubtedly a copy of the Great Stone Bridge but only about half its length. The balustrades, dated 1507, show details closely akin to earlier wooden balustrades, and are interesting examples of the transition from the early more "wooden" forms to the type prevalent in the Ming and Ch'ing dynasties. The panels in the lower portion of the slabs show reliefs of interesting design.

As with buildings, bridge design also became standardized in the Ch'ing dynasty (fig. 78d). There are numerous bridges of the official style in the neighborhood of Peking. The most famous is the Lu-kou Ch'iao, known as the Marco Polo Bridge, which was originally built at the end of the twelfth century during the Ming-ch'ang period of the Chin dynasty. But the present structure of eleven arches, about 1000 feet long over-all, is an eighteenth-century replacement after the original bridge was swept away by a flood. It is the historical site where the Japanese army suddenly attacked the Chinese garrison in a "maneuver" in 1937, known as the Lu-kou Ch'iao Incident, which led to the Sino-Japanese war (fig. 78e).

Arched bridges in southern China are generally lighter in construction than those of the official style. The thirteen-arched bridge of Chin-hua, Chekiang Province, is a superb example (fig. 78f). Bridges of stone piers, spanned by timber girders and with covered roadways, are very common in the south. A typical example is the Bridge at Fu-min, Yunnan Province. Bridges with pillars built of stone drums, also spanned by timber, are found over the rivers Ch'an and Pa, near Sian, Shensi Province (figs. 78g, h). Bridges of enormous stone slabs are not uncommon in the province of Fukien. The suspension bridge is widely used in Szechuan, Kweichow, Yunnan, and Sikang (figs. 78i, j).

78
Bridges
a
An-chi Ch'iao (Great Stone
Bridge), near Chao Hsien,
Hopei, Sui, 581–618

b
An-chi Ch'iao, plan, elevation, and section

c
Yung-t'ung Ch'iao (Little Stone Bridge), Chao Hsien, Hopei, late twelfth century, elevation

河北趙縣 安濟橋（大石橋）
隋李春建

AN-CHI CH'IAO, THE "GREAT STONE BRIDGE"
CHAO HSIEN, HOPEI.
SUI DYNASTY, 589–617 A.D., LI CH'UN, MASTER BUILDER.
OLDEST BRIDGE EXISTING IN CHINA.

SCALE FOR ELEVATION & SECTION
立面断面縮尺

PRESENT RIVER BED   实测時狀況面   R.=27.70 M.
西面立面 WEST ELEVATION

CLEAR SPAN 37.47 M.

關帝閣（元?）
TOWER OF KUANTI
(Yuan Dynasty?)

碑廊（清）
GALLERY OF STELES
(18th Century)

平面圖 PLAN

断面圖 SECTION

平面縮尺 SCALE FOR PLAN

河北趙縣 永通橋
俗呼小石橋·金明昌閒
襄錢而建

25.52 M.

YUNG-T'UNG CH'IAO OR LITTLE STONE BRIDGE
CHAO HSIEN, HOPEI, MING-CH'ANG PERIOD, 1190–95, CHIN DYNASTY.

78
Bridges
d
Ch'ing rules for constructing
a three-arched bridge

e
Lu-kou Ch'iao (Marco Polo
Bridge), Peking, eighteenth
century
f
Thirteen-arched bridge,
Chin-hua, Chekiang, 1694

陝西長安縣 灞河橋
清道光十四年建

BRIDGE OVER PA RIVER, CH'ANG-AN, SHENSI.
CH'ING DYNASTY, 1834 A.D.

石軸柱

STONE DRUMS

斷面畫 CROSS SECTION

測面畫 ELEVATION (1 BAY)

MEASURED BY CHANG C.H

78
Bridges
g
Bridge over Pa River, Sian,
Shensi, 1834, elevation and
section
h
Detail of Pa River bridge

i
Bamboo suspension bridge,
Kuan Hsien, Szechuan, 1803
j
Kuan Hsien suspension bridge,
elevation, plan, and section

Terraces

The *t'ai*, or terrace, was commonly used for recreation as early as the Shang dynasty. Besides many records of such constructions in ancient chronicles, a great number of ruins of early terraces still exist in northern China. Notable among them are the more than a dozen *t'ai*, at the site of the capital of the Kingdom of Yen (second half of the third century B.C.), near I Hsien, Hopei Province. But they are now nothing but large loess platforms, about twenty or thirty feet high, whose original appearance can in no way be reconstructed.

A terrace used for religious purposes is called a *t'an*, or altar. The most illustrious is the Yuan-ch'iu of the Temple of Heaven (commonly known as the Altar of Heaven), Peking, where the emperor made his annual offerings to heaven at dawn on New Year's Day. Established in 1420, it was radically repaired in 1754. The circular marble structure is built up of three tiers, diminishing in diameter, each surrounded by balustrades and approached by steps from four sides (fig. 79a). Other altars in this vicinity, such as those of the Temple of the Earth, or the Temple of Agriculture, are merely low, plain terraces without embellishment.

A terrace of little architectural interest but of great interest to the student of ancient astronomy is the so-called Ts'e-ching T'ai, or Star Observing Terrace of Kao-ch'eng Chen, near Teng-feng, Honan Province (fig. 79b). It is one of the nine terraces built by Kuo Shou-ching in the Yuan dynasty for observing the angle of the sun on the longest and shortest days of the year.

79
Terraces
a
Altar of Heaven (Yuan-ch'iu),
at Temple of Heaven, Peking,
1420, repaired 1754.

河南登封縣告成鎮
測景台 元郭守敬建

CH'ÊH-CHING T'AI, KAO-CH'ENG CHEN,
TENG-FENG, HONAN
AN OBSERVATORY OF THE YUAN DYNASTY
CIRCA 1300 A.D

北

6尺5 0 10M.
平面縮尺 SCALE FOR PLAN

劉敦楨測繪

MEASURED BY LIU T.T.

b

Ts'e-ching T'ai, a Yuan
observatory, Kao-ch'eng Chen,
near Teng-feng, Sung Shan,
Honan, ca. 1300

P'ai-lou Gateways

The *p'ai-lou* is a characteristic Chinese feature that, like the Han paired *ch'üeh* piers, dignified an entrance. As an open symbolic gateway it perhaps owed something to Indian influence, having more than a passing resemblance to the gateways at the famous Sanchi stupa of 25 B.C.

The oldest existing *p'ai-lou* is perhaps the one in Lung-hsing Ssu, Cheng-ting, Hopei Province. It is possibly of the Sung dynasty, but the upper part is very much altered by later restorations. Somewhat similar gateways, called *wu-t'ou men*, are mentioned in the *Ying-tsao fa-shih*, and the term is seen often in T'ang dynasty literature. However, the structure did not become very popular until the Ming dynasty.

The most monumental of its kind is the marble *p'ai-lou* (1540) at the head of the avenue of the Ming Tombs, Ch'ang-p'ing, Hopei Province (fig. 80a). Similar but smaller structures were also erected before some of the tombs of the Ch'ing emperors. Stone *p'ai-lou* in other parts of the country, literally innumerable, can be quite different in character. The five related *p'ai-lou* near Kuang-han, Szechuan Province, are individually typical but a fairly unusual and very impressive sight as a group (fig. 80b).

Wooden *p'ai-lou* are common in Peking. A street *p'ai-lou* and one in front of the lake at the Summer Palace are quite typical (figs. 80c, d). Brick masonry arches, embellished with the form of a *p'ai-lou* in glazed terra-cotta, are also a common sight in Peking (fig. 80e).

80

P'ai-lou Gateways

a

Marble *p'ai-lou*, at entrance to Ming Tombs, Ch'ang-p'ing, Hopei, 1540

b

Five related *p'ai-lou*, near Kuang-han, Szechuan

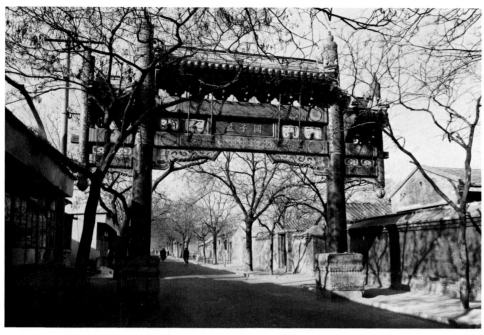

c
Street *p'ai-lou*, Peking
d
Lakefront *p'ai-lou*, Summer
Palace, Peking
e
Glazed terra-cotta *p'ai-lou*,
Kuo-tzu Chien, Peking

Chinese Dynasties and Periods Cited in the Text

Shang–Yin Dynasty	ca. 1766–ca. 1122 B.C.
Chou Dynasty	ca. 1122–221 B.C.
Warring States Period	403–221 B.C.
Ch'in Dynasty	221–206 B.C.
Han Dynasty	206 B.C. –220 A.D.
Eastern Han	25–220
Six Dynasties	ca. 220–581
Northern Wei Period	386–534
Northern Ch'i Period	550–577
Sui Dynasty	581–618
T'ang Dynasty	618–907
Five Dynasties	907–960
(Northern) Sung Dynasty	960–1126
Liao Dynasty	947–1125 (in North China)
(Southern) Sung Dynasty	1127–1279
Chin Dynasty	1115–1234 (in North China)
Yuan Dynasty (Mongol)	1279–1368
Ming Dynasty	1368–1644
Ch'ing Dynasty (Manchu)	1644–1912
Republic	1912–1949
Sino-Japanese War	1937–1945
People's Republic	1949–

Glossary of Technical Terms

Note that the Chinese language does not distinguish between singular and plural. For a guide to pronunciation see the following section.

"accounted heart"	see *chi-hsin*
an 庵	convent
ang 昂	a long slanted lever arm balanced on the *lu-tou*. Its "tail" bears the load of a purlin and is counterbalanced by the eave load at the lower end, in T'ang and Sung construction
ch'a-shou 叉手	truss arms abutting the ridge pole or topmost purlin
che-wu 折屋	the method of "bending the roof"
ch'en-fang t'ou 襯枋頭	a small tie beam above the *hua-kung*
chien-chu 建築	architecture
chi-hsin 計心	a bracket tier or "jump" with complete crossed arms (*kung*); literally, "accounted heart." Cf. *t'ou-hsin*
ch'i 契	a six-*fen* gap or filler between two *ts'ai*
ch'iao 橋	bridge
chih 櫍	transitional disc-shaped member, bronze or stone, between base and foot of column
chien 間	bay
chin-kang pao-tso t'a 金剛寶座塔	five pagodas on a common base, derived from India
ching-chuang 經幢	Dhanari column: freestanding small Buddhist monument in form of column or pagoda
ch'ing-mien ang 琴面昂	"lute-face" *ang* (with pulvinated concave-bevel beak)
chu 柱	column
chu ch'u 柱礎	column base or plinth
chu-ju-chu 侏儒柱	small king post; literally, "dwarf post"
chü-che 舉折	Sung term: method of determining the pitch and curvature of a roof; literally, "raise/depress"
chü-chia 舉架	Ch'ing term: method of determining the pitch and curvature of a roof; literally, "raising the frame"

chü-kao　舉高	the height of a curved roof from the lowest to the highest purlin
chuan-chien　攢尖	pyramidal roof
ch'uan　椽	rafter
ch'üeh　闕	paired gate piers (commonly of Han date)
ch'ung-kung　重栱	two arms forming a double tier to support a lintel
Dhanari column	see *ching-chuang*
fang　枋	small beam or lintel
fang-ch'eng ming-lou　方城明樓	memorial shrine on a high square-walled bastion before a tomb (Ming or Ching)
fen　分	the basic Sung unit for measuring a *ts'ai* (module). One *ts'ai* is 15 *fen* high and ten *fen* wide
feng-shui　風水	geomantic influences; literally, wind and water
fu-chiao lu-tou　附角櫨斗	a grouping of *lu-tou* on the plate (*p'u-p'ai fang*) to strengthen a corner. Adjacent to the corner *lu-tou*, an additional *lu-tou* is added in each of the two directions. One of several techniques for extending complex bracket support around a corner.
fu-tien　廡殿	hip roof
"full ts'ai"	see *tsu-ts'ai*
"grasshopper head"	see *ma-cha t'ou*
hsieh-shan　歇山	gable and hip roof
hsuan-shan　懸山	overhanging gable roof
hua-kung　華栱	bracket extending forward and back from the *lu-tou*, at right angles to the wall plane
jen-tzu kung　人字栱	inverted-V bracket
"jump"	see *t'iao*
ke　閣	multi-storied pavilion
kuan　觀	Taoist temple
kung　宮	palace
kung　栱	bracket arm: bow-shaped timber, set in a bearing block. It supports a smaller block at each upraised end and often in the center.
lan-e　闌額	lintel or architrave
lang　廊	roofed open corridor usually connecting two buildings
liang　樑	beam
ling　檁	purlin
ling-chiao ya-tzu　菱角牙子	chevron-corbelled cornice, on brick pagoda

lou 樓	a building of two or more stories
lu-tou 櫨斗	the principal bearing block, lowest in a bracket set
ma-cha t'ou 螞蚱頭	Ch'ing term: shape of beam end; literally, "grasshopper head"
miao 廟	temple (general term)
ming-fu 明栿	exposed beam
ming-pan 皿板	Han term: a square board beneath the *lu-tou*
p'ai-lou 牌樓	freestanding high gateway, joined overhead
pi-tsang 壁藏	wall sutra cabinet
p'i-chu ang 劈竹昂	"split bamboo *ang*" (with straight-vevel beak)
p'ing-tso 平座	mezzanine story or balcony
pu 步	Ch'ing term: step, the distance from purlin to purlin
p'u-p'ai fang 普拍枋	plate supporting the bracket sets and resting on the lintel, with which it forms a T-shaped cross section
san-fu yun 三福雲	cloud-cluster decoration
sha 刹	finial, atop pagoda
shan-men 山門	main gate of a temple
shu-chu 蜀柱	king post
shu-mi-tso 須彌座	high base with decorated mouldings
shu-yao 束腰	narrow dado in a *shu-mi-tso*
shua-t'ou 耍頭	head of the beam (protruding)
ssu 寺	Buddhist temple
"stolen heart"	see *t'ou-hsin*
stupa	Indian term: Buddhist burial shrine
t'a 塔	pagoda
t'ai 臺	platform or terrace
tan-kung 單栱	one tier of *kung* to support a lintel
t'an 壇	ceremonial terrace or altar
ti-kung 地宮	tomb chamber; literally, "underground palace"
t'i-mu 替木	a narrow member inserted in the *lu-tou* as an auxiliary half-*kung* to support the bracket arm. Also sometimes functions as an arm above a bracket set.
t'iao 跳	an upward projection or tier of a bracket set outward or inward; literally, "jump"
tien 殿	monumental hall
t'ien-hua 天花	ceiling

t'ing-tzu 亭子   small pavilion

to-tien 朵殿   smaller detached side halls of a structure on the same axis; literally, "ear halls"

t'o-chiao 托脚   slanting members bracing individual purlins. See fig. 4

tou 斗   bearing block

tou-k'ou 斗口   in an intercolumnar bracket set, the opening in the *lu-tou* to receive the *kung*; literally, "block mouth." Its width is the basic module in Ch'ing dynasty construction. Cf. *ts'ai*.

tou-kung 斗栱   bracket set

t'ou-hsin 偷心   a bracket tier or "jump" with *kung* in one direction only; literally, "stolen heart." Cf. *chi-hsin*

ts'ai 材   a standard-sized timber used for the *kung*; also, module for measurement in the Sung dynasty. Cf. *tou-k'ou*.

tsao-ching 藻井   caisson ceiling

ts'ao-fu 草栿   rough beam concealed above the ceiling

tsu-ts'ai 足材   a "full *ts'ai*," namely a standard 15- × 10-*fen ts'ai* increased in height by a 6-*fen ch'i*, making a *tsu-ts'ai* 21- × -10-*fen*

tsuan-chien 攢尖   pyramidal roof

wen-fang t'a 文風塔   good luck tower for examination aspirants

wu-liang tien 無梁殿   beamless hall (barrel-vaulted brick structure)

wu-t'ou men 烏頭門   gateway of two or four uprights without a cross beam or roof

yen 檐   eave

ying shan 硬山   flush gable roof

yüeh-liang 月樑   slightly arched beam; literally, "crescent-moon beam"

Guide to Pronunciation

The two Englishmen who produced the Wade-Giles system for romanizing the sounds of Chinese were naturally thinking of English-language equivalents. Thus a non-Chinese-speaking American or Briton can approximate to some degree Chinese pronunciations by following the W-G spelling. For this we must think of each word as having two parts, initial and final. For certain initial consonants, the aspirate is a signal to breathe out naturally when sounding: for example, p' and t'. Without the aspirate, the signal is: withhold the breath to produce the related but stifled sounds b and d. The initials to which this system is applied are:

p'	= p	p	= b
t'	= t	t	= d
k'	= k	k	= g
ch'	= ch	ch	= j
tz'	= tz	tz	= dz

The vowel sounds are the key to the finals. A selected list is given here.

a	= ah	*t'a*	= (tah) pagoda
		ang	= (ahng) slanting lever
ai	= ī	*t'ai*	= (tie) platform
ao	= ow	*miao*	= (cat-call) temple
e	= u, in up	*men*	= (mun) gate, door
final e silent		*ke*	= (g) high pavilion
i	= ee	*pi*	= (bee) pen
ie	= yeh	*tien*	= (dyen) monumental hall
ei	= ay	*nei*	= (nay) inside
ui	= way	*hui*	= (hway) understand
o	= aw	*fo*	= (faw) Buddha
ou	= ō	*tou*	= (doe) bracket block
u	= oo	*kung*	= (goong) bracket arm
final u silent in certain cases		*ssu*	= (ss) Buddhist temple

Selected Bibliography

Chinese Sources

Shortened Names of Publishers in Peking

Chien-kung: Chung-kuo chien-chu kung-yeh ch'u-pan-she 中國建築工業出版社 (China Building Industry Press)

Ch'ing-hua: Ch'ing-hua ta-hsueh chien-chu hsi 清華大學建築系 (Tsing Hua University, Department of Architecture)

Wen-wu: Wen-wu ch'u-pan-she 文物出版社 (Cultural Relics Publishing House)

YTHS: Chung-kuo ying-tsao hsueh-she 中國營造學社 (Society for Research in Chinese Architecture)

Publications

Bulletin, Society for Research in Chinese Architecture. See *Chung-kuo ying-tsao hsueh-she hui-k'an*.

Chang Chung-yi 張仲一, Ts'ao Chien-pin 曹見賓, Fu Kao-chieh 傅高傑, Tu Hsiu-chün 杜修均. *Hui-chou Ming-tai chu-chai* 徽州明代住宅 (Ming period houses in Hui-chou [Anhwei]). Peking: Chien-kung, 1957.
A useful study of domestic architecture.

Ch'en Ming-ta 陳明達. *Ying Hsien mu-t'a* 應縣木塔 (The Ying Hsien Wooden Pagoda). Peking: Wen-wu, 1980.
Important text, photographs, and drawings by Liang's former student and colleague. English abstract.

————. *Ying-tsao fa-shih ta-mu-tso yen-chiu* 營造法式大木作研究 (Research on timber construction in the Sung manual *Building Standards*). Peking: Wen-wu, 1981.
A continuation and development of Liang's research.

Ch'en Wen-lan 陳文瀾, ed. *Chung-kuo chien-chu ying-tsao t'u-ch'i* 中國建築營造圖集 (Chinese architectural structure: Illustrated reference manual). Peking: Ch'ing-hua (nei-pu) (內部), 1952. No text; for internal use only.

Chien-chu k'e-hsueh yen-chiu-yuan, Chien-chu li-lun chi li-shih yen-chiu-shih, Chung-kuo chien-chu shih pien-chi wei-yuan-hui 建築科學研究院建築理論研究室中國建築史編輯委員會 (Editorial Committee on the History of Chinese Architecture, Architectural Theory and History Section, Institute of Architectural Science). *Chung-kuo ku-tai chien-chu chien-shih* 中國古代建築簡史 (A summary history of ancient Chinese architecture). Peking: Chien-kung, 1962.

————. *Chung-kuo chin-tai chien-chu chien shih* 中國近代建築簡史 (A summary history of modern Chinese architecture). Peking: Chien-kung, 1962.

Chien-chu kung-ch'eng pu, Chien-chu k'e-hsueh yen-chiu-yuan, Chien-chu li-lun chi li-shih yen-chiu-shih 建築工程部建築科學研究院建築理論及歷史研究室 (Architectural Theory and History Section, Institute of Architectural Science, Ministry of Architectural Engineering). *Pei-ching ku chien-chu* 北京古建築 (Ancient architecture in Peking). Peking: Wen-wu, 1959.
Illustrated with excellent photographs.

Chung-kuo k'e-hsueh yuan T'u-mu chien-chu yen-chiu-so 中國科學院土木建築研究院 (Institute of Engineering and Architecture, Chinese Academy of Sciences), and Ch'ing-hua ta-hsueh Chien-chu hsi 清華大學建築系 (Department of Architecture, Tsing Hua University), comp. *Chung-kuo chien-chu* 中國建築 (Chinese architecture). Peking: Wen-wu, 1957.
Very important text and pictures, supervised by Liang.

Chung-kuo ying-tsao hsueh-she hui-k'an 中國營造學社彙刊 (Bulletin, Society for Research in Chinese Architecture). Peking, 1930–1937, vol. 1, no. 1–vol. 6, no. 4; Li-chuang, Szechuan, 1945. vol. 7, nos. 1–2.

Liang Ssu-ch'eng 梁思成. *Chung-kuo i-shu shih: Chien-chu p'ien ch'a-t'u* 中國藝術史：建築篇插圖 (History of Chinese arts: Architecture volume, illustrations). N.p., n.d., [before 1949].

———, Chang Jui 張銳. *T'ien-chin t'e-pieh-shih wu-chih chien-she fang-an* 天津特別市物質建設方案 (Construction plan for the Tientsin Special City). N.p., 1930.

———, Liu Chih-p'ing 劉致平, comp. *Ch'ien-chu she-chi ts'an-k'ao t'u-chi* 建築設計參考圖集 (Reference pictures for architectural design). 10 vols. Peking: YTHS, 1935–1937.
Important reference volumes treating platforms, stone balustrades, shop fronts, brackets, glazed tiles, pillar bases, outer eave patterns, consoles, and caisson ceilings.

———. *Ch'ing-tai ying-tsao tse-li* 清代營造則例 (Ch'ing structural regulations). Peking: YTHS, 1934; 2nd ed., Peking: Chung-kuo chien-chu kung-yeh ch'u-pan-she, 1981.
Interpretation of text from field studies.

———, ed. *Ying-tsao suan-li* 營造算例 (Calculation rules for Ch'ing architecture). Peking: YTHS, 1934.
The original Ch'ing text of the *Kung-ch'eng tso-fa tse-li*, edited and reorganized by Liang.

———. *Ch'ü-fu K'ung-miao chien-chu chi ch'i hsiu-ch'i chi-hua* 曲阜孔廟建築及其修葺計劃 (The architecture of Confucius' temple in Ch'ü-fu and a plan for its renovation). Peking: YTHS, 1935.

———. *Jen-min shou-tu ti shih-cheng chien-she* 人民首都的市政建設 (City construction in the People's Capital). Peking: Chung-hua ch'uan-kuo k'e-hsueh chi-shu p'u-chi hsieh-hui 中華全國科學技術普及協會, 1952.
Lectures on planning for Peking.

———, ed. *Sung ying-tsao fa-shih t'u-chu* 宋營造法式圖註 (Drawings with annotations of the rules for structural carpentry of the Sung Dynasty). Peking: Ch'ing-hua (nei-pu)（內部）, 1952.
No text; for internal use only.

———, ed. *Ch'ing-shih ying-tsao tse-li t'u-pan* 清式營造則例圖版 (Ch'ing structural regulations: Drawings). Peking: Ch'ing-hua (nei-pu)（內部）, 1952.
No text; for internal use only.

———, ed. *Chung-kuo chien-chu shih t'u-lu* 中國建築史圖錄 (Chinese architectural history: Drawings). Peking: Ch'ing-hua (nei-pu)（內部）, 1952.
No text; for internal use only.

———. *Tsu-kuo ti chien-chu* 祖國的建築 (The Architecture of the Motherland). Peking: Chung-hua ch'uan-kuo k'e-hsueh chi-shu p'u-chi hsieh-hui 中華全國科學技術普及協會, 1954.
A popularization.

———. *Chung-kuo chien-chu shih* 中國建築史 (History of Chinese architecture). Shanghai: Shang-wu yin-shu kuan 商務印書館, 1955.
Photocopy of his major general work, handwritten in wartime, ca. 1943. Published for university textbook use only. Unillustrated.

———. *Ku chien-chu lun-ts'ung* 古建築論叢 (Collected essays on ancient architecture). Hong Kong: Shen-chou t'u-shu kung-ssu 神州圖書公司, 1975.
Includes his study of Fo-kuang Ssu.

———. *Liang Ssu-ch'eng wen-chi* 梁思成文集 (Collected essays of Liang Ssu-ch'eng). Vol. I. Peking: Chien-kung, 1982.
First of projected series of six volumes.

Liu Chih-p'ing 劉致平. *Chung-kuo chien-chu ti lei-hsing chih chieh-ko* 中國建築的類型和結構 (Chinese building types and structure). Peking: Chien-kung, 1957.
Important work by Liang's student and colleague.

Liu Tun-chen [Liu Tun-tseng] 劉敦楨, ed. *P'ai-lou suan-li* 牌樓算例 (Rules of calculation for P'ai-lou). Peking: YTHS, 1933.

———. *Ho-pei sheng hsi-pu ku chien-chu tiao-ch'a chi-lueh* 河北省西部古建築調查紀略 (Brief report on the survey of ancient architecture in Western-Hopei). Peking: YTHS, 1935.

———. *I Hsien Ch'ing Hsi-ling* 易縣清西陵 (Western tombs of the Ch'ing emperors in I Hsien, Hopei). Peking: YTHS, 1935.

———. *Su-chou ku chien-chu tiao-ch'a chi* 蘇州古建築調查記 (A report on the survey of ancient architecture in Soochow). Peking: YTHS, 1936.

————, Liang Ssu-ch'eng 梁思成. *Ch'ing Wen-yuan ke shih-ts'e t'u-shuo* 清文淵閣實測圖說 (Explanation with drawings of the survey of Wen-yuan Ke of the Ch'ing). N.p., n.d. [before 1949].

————. *Chung-kuo chu-chai kai-shuo* 中國住宅概說 (A brief study of Chinese domestic architecture). Peking: Chien-kung, 1957.
Also published in French and Japanese editions.

————, ed. *Chung-kuo ku-tai chien-chu shih* 中國古代建築史 (A history of ancient Chinese architecture). Peking: Chien-kung, 1980.
An important textbook.

————. *Liu Tun-chen wen-chi* 劉敦楨文集 (Collected essays of Liu Tun-chen). Vol. I. Peking: Chien-kung, 1982.

Lu Sheng 盧繩. *Ch'eng-te ku chien-chu* 承德古建築 (Ancient architecture in Chengte). Peking: Chien-kung, n.d. [ca. 1980].

Yao Ch'eng-tsu 姚承祖, Chang Yung-sen 張鏞森. *Ying-tsao fa-yuan* 營造法原 (Rules for building). Peking: Chien-kung n.d. [ca. 1955].
A unique account, written several centuries ago, of construction methods in the Yangtze Valley.

Western-Language Sources

Boerschmann, E. *Chinesische Architektur.* 2 vols. Berlin: Wasmuth, 1925.

Boyd, Andrew. *Chinese Architecture and Town Planning, 1500 B.C.–A.D. 1911.* London: Alec Tiranti, 1962; Chicago: University of Chicago Press, 1962.

Chinese Academy of Architecture, comp. *Ancient Chinese Architecture.* Peking: China Building Industry Press; Hong Kong: Joint Publishing Co., 1982.
Recent color photographs of old buildings, many restored.

Demieville, Paul. "Che-yin Song Li Ming-tchong Ying tsao fa che." *Bulletin, Ecole Française d'Extrême Orient* 25 (1925): 213–264.
Masterly review of the 1920 edition of the Sung manual.

Ecke, Gustav. "The Institute for Research in Chinese Architecture. I. A Short Summary of Field Work Carried on from Spring 1932 to Spring 1937." *Monumenta Serica* 2 (1936–37): 448–474.
Detailed summary by an Institute member.

————. "Chapter I: Structural Features of the Stone-Built T'ing Pagoda. A Preliminary Study." *Monumenta Serica* 1 (1935/1936): 253–276.

————. "Chapter II: Brick Pagodas in the Liao Style." *Monumenta Serica* 13 (1948): 331–365.

Fairbank, Wilma. "The Offering Shrines of 'Wu Liang Tz'u'" and "A Structural Key to Han Mural Art." In *Adventures in Retrieval: Han Murals and Shang Bronze Molds*, pp. 43–86, 89–140. Cambridge, Mass.: Harvard University Press, 1972.

Glahn, Else. "On the Transmission of the *Ying-tsao fa-shih*." *T'oung Pao* 61 (1975): 232–265.

————. "Palaces and Paintings in Sung." In *Chinese Painting and the Decorative Style*, ed. M. Medley. London: Percival David Foundation, 1975. Pp. 39–51.

————. "Some Chou and Han Architectural Terms." *Bulletin No. 50, The Museum of Far Eastern Antiquities* (Stockholm, 1978), pp. 105–118.

————. Glahn, Else. "Chinese Building Standards in the 12th Century." *Scientific American*, May 1981, pp. 162–173.
Discussion of the Sung manual by the leading Western expert. (Edited and illustrated without her participation.)

Liang Ssu-ch'eng. "Open Spandrel Bridges of Ancient China. I. The An-chi Ch'iao at Chao-chou, Hopei." *Pencil Points*, January 1938, pp. 25–32.

————. "Open Spandrel Bridges of Ancient China. II. The Yung-tung Ch'iao at Chao-chou, Hopei." *Pencil Points*, March 1938. pp. 155–160.

————. "China's Oldest Wooden Structure." *Asia Magazine*, July 1941, pp. 387–388.
The first publication on the Fo-kuang Ssu discovery.

————. "Five Early Chinese Pagodas." *Asia Magazine*, August 1941, pp. 450–453.

Needham, Joseph. *Science and Civilization in China.* Vol. 4, part 3: "Civil Engineering and Nautics." Cambridge: Cambridge University Press, 1971. Pp. 58–210.
Exhaustive treatment of Chinese building.

Pirazzoli-t'Serstevens, Michele. *Living Architecture: Chinese*. Translated from French. New York: Grosset and Dunlap, 1971; London: Macdonald, 1972.

Sickman, Laurence, and Soper, Alexander. *The Art and Architecture of China*. Harmondsworth: Penguin, 1956. 3rd ed. 1968; paperback ed. 1971, reprinted 1978.
Still a leading source.

Sirén, Osvald. *The Walls and Gates of Peking*. New York: Orientalia, 1924.

————. *The Imperial Palaces of Peking*. Paris and Brussels: Van Oest, 1926. 3 vols.

Thilo, Thomas. *Klassische chinesische Baukunst: Strukturprinzipien und soziale Function*. Leipzig: Koehler und Amelang, 1977.

Willetts, William. "Architecture." In *Chinese Art*, 2:653–754. New York: George Braziller, 1958.

Index